Investigating Jesus

JOHN DICKSON

Investigating Jesus

An Historian's Quest

LION

A Lion Book
an imprint of
Lion Hudson plc
Wilkinson House, Jordan Hill Road,
Oxford OX2 8DR, England
www.lionhudson.com

ISBN 978 0 7459 5350 2

Distributed by:
UK: Marston Book Services, PO Box 269, Abingdon, Oxon, OX14 4YN
USA: Trafalgar Square Publishing, 814 N. Franklin Street, Chicago, IL 60610
USA Christian Market: Kregel Publications, PO Box 2607, Grand Rapids, MI 49501

First edition 2010
10 9 8 7 6 5 4 3 2 1 0
All rights reserved

Acknowledgments
Scripture taken from the Holy Bible, Today's New International® Version TNIV©.
Copyright 2001, 2005 by International Bible Society®. Used by permission of
International Bible Society®. All rights reserved worldwide.
'TNIV' and 'Today's New International Version' are trademarks registered in the
United States Patent and Trademark Office by International Bible Society®.

A catalogue record for this book is available
from the British Library

Typeset in 11/12 News 702 BT

Printed and bound in Singapore

Contents

Introduction:
Jesus on the Fringe

Recently, I was involved behind the scenes in a public debate on the value of religion in society. I found myself at dinner afterwards sitting opposite one of the key speakers. He had just argued (and won) the motion: 'We would be better off without religion.' So, perhaps inevitably, our conversation soon turned to things religious. 'Scholars agree we know almost nothing about Jesus,' said this professor of physics and author of a recent atheist book. 'That is, if he existed at all,' he added. I asked him if he knew any particular scholars who had argued this. He did. 'Professor Wells of London,' was his reply.

The name Wells is well known to those interested in New Testament history as that of the scholar who thirty years ago published his doubts about Jesus' existence.[1] His most recent claim to fame, however, comes from being cited by Richard Dawkins in his immensely popular book *The God Delusion*. Dawkins presents Wells as an expert who has made a 'serious' historical case that Jesus never lived.[2] What is not mentioned is that George Wells is London University's Professor of German – not history or biblical studies. The fact that Dawkins and my physicist friend both depend on a language professor for information about a figure from first-century Palestine says something about the gap between popular perceptions of Jesus and the views of experts (in the relevant field).

So far as I know, no professional historian – that is, no scholar teaching, researching and publishing in an ancient history department or biblical studies department of a reputable university – thinks that Jesus' existence is still in doubt. Fearing that my own bias might be clouding my judgment, I recently asked three ancient historians, all full professors in Australian universities, if they knew of any professional ancient historian or biblical historian in any university in the world who argues that Jesus never lived. All three drew a blank. One of them was Professor Graeme Clarke, a renowned classicist from the Australian National University and author of the chapter on Christianity in a volume of *The Cambridge Ancient History*[3] (a standard academic reference). He is not a religious man. He replied very forthrightly: 'Frankly, I know of no ancient historian or biblical historian who would have a twinge of doubt about the existence of a Jesus Christ – the documentary evidence is simply overwhelming.'[4] He added, 'You can quote me' – which I have dutifully done.

This book tries to bridge the gap between popular perception and scholarly judgment about the figure of Jesus. In particular, it tries to unpack *how* scholars in the discipline reach their judgments. But, first, I should clarify which 'discipline' I am talking about. This is not a book about theology, the study of God (which Dawkins considers a non-discipline).[5] It is entirely about history and, in particular, New Testament history. It will perhaps surprise readers to learn that this field is populated by literally thousands of academics working in history departments and biblical studies departments in universities throughout the world. Some of these scholars do have some kind of Christian faith, but plenty of others have no faith. Still others are professing Jews, who are experts on Jesus because of their knowledge of first-century Palestine. The important thing to note, though, is that all of them know not to employ faith arguments in their work. The Christians never use the approach, 'The Bible says it, so it must be true.' Likewise, the atheists – and there are a few in the field – know not to resort to sceptical propaganda. From top to bottom this is a *secular* enterprise. It is an attempt to understand the man Jesus using only the tools of historical criticism.

Key here is the protocol known as 'peer review'. To become part of the expert conversation, scholars publish their research in a reputable academic journal or book series (of which there are well over a hundred in this field). This involves submitting work to at least two academic peers, not connected with the author, who will assess whether it makes a potential contribution to the field. If it passes, it is published and discussed more widely. If not, it sits forlornly somewhere on the scholar's hard drive (I have had both success and disappointment

Christ Bearing the Cross, c. 1550–1560, by Luis de Morales.

here). Throughout this book I will occasionally refer to 'mainstream scholars'. By this I mean scholars who are part of this academic conversation. Some scholars (and popular writers) sit on the margins of this conversation (such as George Wells), generally avoiding the peer-review process and publishing directly to the unsuspecting public. Often what they say is exciting, ranging from 'Jesus never lived' to 'He had a wife and three children'. But such views are not taken seriously by mainstream scholars. It is partly because of the sensationalist nature of these 'marginal' books and DVDs that there is so much confusion in the general public about the Jesus of history.

The gap between popular writing on Jesus and the opinion of the experts finds a partial analogy in the climate-change debate. Over the last twenty years an overwhelming body of data has convinced most scientists that global warming is a serious problem and is, in part, the result of human industrial activity. Points of dispute remain, but there is a clear mainstream consensus that the issue is significant enough to warrant wide-ranging efforts to redress the situation. In the last few years the general public has caught up with this scholarly consensus. Most people, whether expert or lay, now accept that climate change is a potentially hazardous reality.

You will, however, still find the occasional scientist who challenges these mainstream conclusions. Coincidentally, as I was writing this, Australia's national broadcaster, the ABC, aired the 'controversial' British documentary *The Great Global Warming Swindle*, which challenges the scientific consensus, insisting that the 'warming' we observe is a natural phenomenon, not the result of our carbon emissions. Imagine for a moment if this sceptical message were the only one we heard over the next ten years or so. I suspect our perception of what scientists thought about global warming would slowly become skewed by those voices from the fringes of science. Only those of us game enough to read *Nature* or the *Journal of Ecology* would realize how marginal these voices really were.

Fortunately, this is never going to happen with an issue like climate change. The scientific data are too compelling and the stakes too high. The consequences of ignoring the evidence are so great that government bodies and educational institutions will now never allow the 'global warming sceptics' to have the last word. Mainstream science is thus guaranteed its rightful voice. Interestingly, straight after the airing of *The Great Global Warming Swindle* the ABC thought it wise to host a live panel discussion of expert scientists. Those interested enough to listen to the discussion, which was considerably less gripping than what preceded it, were left in no doubt as to the fringe nature of the documentary's arguments.

In historical Jesus studies, as with environmental science, there is a large mainstream consensus. Over the last thirty years historical scholars have inched towards something resembling a consensus about the man from Nazareth, certainly concerning the major details of his life. One of the leading scholars of the last couple of decades is Professor Ed Sanders of Duke University. He is no friend of Christian apologetics and thinks nothing of dismissing parts of the biblical narrative if they do not fit with his historical analysis. Yet even he can summarize the scholarly situation in words that may surprise some readers: 'There are no substantial doubts about the general course of Jesus' life: when and where he lived, approximately when and where he died, and the sort of thing that he did during his public activity.'[6] This statement would be accepted by all leading Jesus scholars working in the field today.

Despite this broad consensus, popular controversialists continue to talk as if everything were up for grabs. For example, Christopher Hitchens, the noted journalist and author of the provocative *God is Not Great*, can speak of 'the highly questionable existence of Jesus'.[7] French atheist Michel Onfray goes further: 'Jesus's existence has not been historically established. No contemporary documentation of the event, no archaeological proof, nothing certain exists today... We must leave it to lovers of impossible debates to decide on the question of Jesus's existence.'[8] The result of all this is a skewing of the public's perception of what mainstream experts think.

This is where my analogy with the global warming issue breaks down. In the historical Jesus debate it is the *fringe*, not the mainstream, that gets most of the airtime. The national

Marble bust of Emperor Augustus, who ruled the empire c. 27 BC–AD 14. It was during his reign that Jesus was born.

broadcasters of the world are unlikely to follow up their controversial documentaries about Jesus with a panel discussion of leading historians. There is neither the interest nor the sense of importance; no ecosystems hang in the balance.

Christian churches, of course, feel the importance and hit back with their apologetic resources – books and DVDs attempting to answer every criticism and neutralize every whiff of scepticism. Such works are often as marginal as the nay-saying books and documentaries (though never as popular). In fact, the two are often the mirror image of each other. Apologetic writers search for evidence to prove Christianity, while sceptical authors go looking for arguments to disprove it. The one side resorts to special pleading, the other to cheap spoiling. Both make for bad history, which is why neither tends to publish in the hundred or so academic journals devoted to the subject.

Mainstream scholars, on the other hand, avoid special pleading and spoiling. Their aim is neither to prove nor to disprove the Christian faith. They approach the evidence about Jesus the same way they approach the data about Alexander the Great, Julius Caesar, or the Emperor Nero. They do not elevate the New Testament as a sacred volume, but nor do they dismiss it as a spurious collection of myths. There is a respect towards the writings of the first Christians, but there is no reverence.

Controversial books and documentaries about Jesus make for good news stories and often become bestsellers, but they do nothing to bring clarity. We do not need more sensational works on Jesus; we need ones that deliberately try to narrow the gap – a gap recently bridged on the climate-change issue – between academic consensus and popular perception. My small contribution to that effort is to try to explain in straightforward language *how* mainstream historians arrive at their conclusions about Jesus. What sources do they use? What methods do they employ? How rigorous is the whole process?

Let me begin, though, by briefly telling the story of 2,000 years of research into the life of Jesus.

1

The Quest for Jesus from Beginnings to the Enlightenment

Academic tomes on this subject – which this is not – often begin their account of the search for the historical Jesus by reaching back only as far as the eighteenth to nineteenth centuries. They introduce readers to the great German scholars Hermann Reimarus and David Strauss and their attempts to apply the critical insights of the Enlightenment to the study of the central religious figure of Western history. But historical questions about Jesus were raised long before the Enlightenment; the modern era was not the first to wonder how much of the story was really true. (It is the conceit of every age to think that it has discovered the most important questions – and answers.)

The quest for the historical Jesus in fact began almost as soon as he left the scene in AD 30.

The ancient quest

Even the author of one of the four New Testament Gospels shows an interest in searching out the facts rather than mere opinions about the man from Nazareth. The Gospel of Luke opens with these telling words:

Many have undertaken to draw up an account of the things that have been fulfilled among us, just as they were handed down to us by those who from the first were eyewitnesses and servants of the word. With this in mind, since I myself have carefully investigated everything from the beginning, I too decided to write an orderly account for you, most excellent Theophilus, so that you may know the certainty of the things you have been taught.

Luke 1:1–4

Whatever else this is, it is the statement of someone committed to weighing earlier sources, gathering (eyewitness) testimony, researching thoroughly and then providing an orderly account of the most reliable data. This sounds more like history than theology.

A depiction of Luke by Simon Vouet (1590–1649).

Professor Richard Bauckham of Scotland's famous University of St Andrew's – famous for its scholarship as well as for being Prince William's *alma mater* – has recently shown that Luke's declared interest in 'those who from the first were eyewitnesses' is strongly reminiscent of other historical writers in ancient times, including Polybius, Dionysis of Halicarnassus and the first-century Jewish writer Josephus. When I interviewed Bauckham for a recent television documentary he spoke of various 'features in the Gospels which reveal just how keen these biblical writers were to preserve trustworthy testimony about Jesus, and *eyewitness* testimony in particular'.[1] I asked him if we can take seriously Luke's claim to depend on the testimony of *autoptai*, 'eyewitnesses'. 'Yes, I think we should,' he replied, in no uncertain terms, 'because it connects very easily with the way historians in the ancient world viewed the writing of history. They actually thought you could only really write contemporary history – history within the lifetime of people who had been involved participants in the events.' He then added this very important observation:

> And it is also interesting that what Luke actually does is describe them as the eyewitnesses and 'ministers of the word', which implies that these eyewitnesses had a role in the early Christian communities. They were ministers of the word, that is, they were giving their eyewitness testimony. They were the people whom someone like Luke, but also quite ordinary Christians or Christian preachers, would look to as authoritative sources for knowing about Jesus. These people were not just people who had been eyewitnesses but then thirty years later Luke comes along and asks them; they were actually people who had been telling their testimony all the time.[2]

The survival of biblical scholarship

It is fair to say that biblical scholarship suffered greatly between about AD 500 and 1500. Christian North Africa (where Augustine lived and worked) fell to the Vandals in the mid-fifth century. Centres of Christian learning, such as Alexandria (in Egypt), Palestine, and Asia Minor (Turkey), were lost in the seventh century with the triumph of Islam. Now biblical scholarship (of a more dogmatic kind) was kept alive in monasteries by philosophical theologians such as Peter Abelard (1079–1142), Hugh of Saint-Victor (1096–1141) and Thomas Aquinas (1225–1274). Christian monasteries were the forerunners of the modern university. It should also be noted that a rich scholarly tradition – for the Old Testament – existed among medieval Jews. The towering figure here is Moses Maimonides (1135–1204), also known as Rambam, an acronym for his full Hebrew name Rabbi Moshe ben Maimon. His expertise ranged across many disciplines, including linguistics, scriptural interpretation, archaeology, philosophy and medicine.

The idea that the Gospel writers were interested in 'spiritual truths' rather than historical events is as false as it is out of date.[3]

By the second century, the New Testament Gospels were widely read and revered by Christians all over the Roman empire and beyond. Indeed, it seems that one of the methods of *Christianizing* the world at that time was to distribute the four Gospels.[4] Wherever there were Christians in this period there were Gospels, and wherever there were Gospels there were people becoming Christians.

However, we must not think that this reverence for the Gospels led all Christians to approach their sacred books with pre-scientific blind faith. Intellectuals like the famous Origen of Caesarea (AD 185–253) were as meticulous in analysing the Gospels as anything we observe in modern scholarship. His approach is worth detailing.[5]

Origen lived in a period of intense criticism of Christianity. While he was still a teenager, his father was martyred for the faith, an event that would have a huge impact on this brilliant young scholar. He threw himself into his studies, not only of classical subjects like Greek grammar, mathematics, rhetoric, history and philosophy, but also of Christian theology. And when he turned to the Gospels, as he did time and time again during his fifty-year academic career, he was relentless in his analysis.

Origen consulted as many manuscripts as he could find, in order to reconstruct the most accurate form of the text: today we call this 'textual criticism'. He assessed the geography of the Gospels against his own personal knowledge of Palestine, something archaeologists are still doing. Perhaps most impressively, he carefully compared the four Gospels and honestly noted the differences between them. He did not try to harmonize the accounts into one neat version of the Jesus story, as others had done;[6] rather, he wanted to discern each Gospel writer's particular emphasis and editorial hand. Scholars today call this 'redaction criticism'. Sometimes Origen made judgments about the details of the Gospels that would make conservative Christians today a little queasy. And yet he remained a firm believer to the end, absolutely committed to reading the whole Bible as the Word of God. It was precisely Origen's faith in the God of truth that fuelled his commitment to search for the truth about Jesus.

If this were a different sort of book, we could devote many more pages to exploring the work of scholars in ancient and medieval times who applied their significant intellectual powers to a rigorous analysis of the Gospels and Jesus. Among the stars of the story would be Eusebius of Caesarea (260–339), Jerome (331–420), John Chrysostom (347–407) and Augustine (354–430); and at the dawn of the modern period, Desiderius Erasmus (1469–1536) and Martin Luther (1483–1546).

A 1584 engraving of the Christian scholar, Origen (AD 185–253).

Perhaps Origen's greatest contribution to early scholarship was his production of the Hexapla, a six-column version of the Old Testament. In the left-hand column was the Hebrew text used by Palestinian Jews. Next to that was a Greek transliteration of the Hebrew, indicating (for those not quite the polymath Origen was) the correct pronunciation of the Hebrew words. In the remaining columns were four well-known Greek translations of the Hebrew Bible, one or two of them dating to several centuries earlier and used widely by Greek-speaking Jews. Origen's aim in all this was to assess the most accurate version of the Old Testament as a basis for dialogue between Jews and Christians. Historians regard the Hexapla as a marvel of scholarship – by ancient or modern standards.

With due respect to the towering figures of medieval scholarship, I want to move forward to one of the most significant periods in human history – a period that would change for ever how we studied Jesus.

The First Quest: the confidence of the Enlightenment

The 'Enlightenment' was a European intellectual movement of the seventeenth and eighteenth centuries which emphasized the power of human reason to discover what was valuable in life. Buoyed by the significant artistic, technical and scientific successes of the recent Renaissance period (1400s–1500s), Enlightenment thinkers felt free to question everything. They would not be constrained by mere tradition, whether cultural or ecclesiastical. The consequences for biblical studies were significant.

Whereas earlier scholarship was inspired by its faith in Christian teachings, Enlightenment scholarship was guided by its confidence in human reason. In truth, neither approach lacked the application of reason, as the example of Origen amply demonstrates, and neither really lacked a faith commitment either. As contemporary philosophers remind us, the basis for all intellectual enquiry is a *trust*, faith, in one's rational powers.[7]

Enlightenment scholarship was absolutely confident in its ability to separate fact from fiction in the Bible. It could do this using linguistics, historiography, archaeology and philosophy,

without recourse to the 'dogmas' of the Christian church. Many have called this movement the 'First Quest' for the historical Jesus. Some of the key figures and ideas of this quest follow.

The 'revolutionary Jesus' of Hermann Samuel Reimarus (1694–1768)

German scholar Hermann Reimarus epitomized the Enlightenment spirit and in some ways can be said to have launched the First Quest for Jesus. Reimarus was a professor of oriental languages in Hamburg and a thoroughgoing 'Deist'; he believed in some kind of Creator but rejected the idea that God had revealed himself to humanity (whether in the Bible or elsewhere).[8] It was out of this philosophical perspective that he wrote his stinging critique

of orthodox Christianity titled 'Apologia or Defence of the Rational Worshippers of God'. He originally made it available only to a close circle of friends. However, after his death, sections of the work were published by the philosopher G. E. Lessing. These included chapters titled 'On the Resurrection Narratives' and 'On the Intentions of Jesus and His Disciples'.[9]

Reimarus insisted that we must distinguish between what Jesus actually said and did and what the apostles merely claimed he said and did. In other words, he posited a significant difference, even contradiction, between the 'Jesus of history' and the 'Christ of faith', which he saw as a construct of the early church. The historical Jesus was a political revolutionary, Reimarus thought, who was only transformed by later Christians into a universal saviour. Many echo this sentiment today without realizing where it comes from.

The 'mythical Jesus' of David Friedrich Strauss (1808–1874)

Reimarus' extreme scepticism and anti-Christian agenda were cemented (if slightly moderated) by another German Enlightenment scholar, David Strauss. One of the most influential books of the nineteenth century, Strauss's *The Life of Jesus Critically Examined* (published in 1835–36),[10] argued that the Gospels needed to be understood as myth. 'Myth' here does not mean simply untrue; nor did Strauss go along with Reimarus in thinking that the apostles set out deliberately to deceive. What he meant was that wherever the Gospel writers strain our rational minds – as in the miracle stories – they are employing the religious imagination to express the inexpressible longings of the human soul. The resurrection narratives, for instance, are not lies. Nor are they history. They are rather poetical images (myths) of the divine life which the early Christians longed for.

Unlike Reimarus, David Strauss believed that the core ideas of Christianity – peace and love and so on – could still be preserved and enjoyed even if the main events were not true. A modern theologian in the Straussian mode is the popular US writer Bishop John Shelby Spong.[11]

The 'wise man Jesus' of Joseph Ernest Renan (1823–1892)

David Strauss launched a flurry of very confident critical analyses of the life of Jesus. In 1863 the French philosopher and historian Ernest Renan published his *Life of Jesus* in which he cast Jesus as a charming and wise Galilean preacher whose initial popularity soon waned – to the point of rejection – on account of the high demands he placed on his followers.[12]

The First Quest was beginning to take a particular shape. Jesus as the simple, wise teacher would become a stock theme in many discussions about him (even today).

David Friedrich Strauss (1808–1874), German theologian and philosopher.

The 'non-Messiah Jesus' of William Wrede (1859–1906)

In the latter half of the nineteenth century there was still some confidence in two basic historical 'facts': first, that Mark's Gospel (if none of the others) was a broadly accurate account of Jesus' life, and secondly, that Jesus himself had claimed to be the Messiah. Both of these propositions, however, were dealt a major blow in 1901 with the publication of *The Messianic Secret* by William Wrede of the University of Breslau (Polish Wroclaw).[13]

Wrede drew attention to the fact that in Mark's Gospel Jesus occasionally asks people not to tell others that he is the Messiah. He further noted that the New Testament frequently ties Jesus' messianic credentials *not* to his earthly ministry but to his supposed resurrection from the dead.[14] From this Wrede surmised that Jesus himself never suggested he was the Messiah (he was simply a great teacher). The messianic idea was invented by the disciples after Jesus' death and then written back into the story *retrospectively*. Because Jesus' contemporaries knew he never made claims to messiahship, Wrede continued, Mark had to invent a supplementary idea to explain Jesus' apparent silence on the matter: Jesus revealed his identity only to his closest disciples, asking them to keep it a secret until after his death and resurrection. In this way, so the argument went, the early Christians turned a noble preacher into the glorious Messiah.

Albert Schweitzer (1875–1965) and the end of the Enlightenment quest

The strident scepticism of Enlightenment scholars from Reimarus to Wrede must have seemed unstoppable. The power of human reason seemed to have triumphed over the fancies of the Christian faith. But the confidence was ill-placed. Within a decade of William Wrede's 1901 publication – and within two centuries of the start of the Enlightenment project – the rationalist quest for Jesus would collapse before the work of a man who, as one modern scholar puts it, 'stands at the head of the [twentieth] century like a colossus'.[15]

Albert Schweitzer was a supremely gifted philosopher, historian and theologian, as well as being an accomplished musician. After publishing some of the most significant books on the New Testament ever written (and one on the music of J. S. Bach, for good measure), he left academia, completed a medical degree and devoted himself to medical missionary work in Gabon, West Africa. This 'jungle surgeon' won the Nobel Peace Prize in 1952 and, true to form, gave the prize money to a leper hospital.

In 1906 Schweitzer published *The Quest of the Historical Jesus*.[16] It was a stunning critique of the previous 150 years of research from Reimarus to Wrede.[17] He ably demonstrated that the portraits of Jesus offered by these supposedly objective historians were basically 'projections' of their own ethical ideals. The characterization of Jesus as a simple, noble teacher, for instance, does not arise from the evidence, he argued, but is a construct born of the humanism of the Enlightenment. Such a Jesus is a figment of the scholarly imagination; or, as Schweitzer himself put it, 'a figure designed by rationalism, endowed with life by liberalism, and clothed by modern theology in an historical garb'.[18] (Ouch!) It was a simple observation,

Dr Albert Schweitzer (1875–1965), world-famous biblical scholar and physician, stands outside one of the buildings of his hospital at Lambarene in Gabon, Africa, December 1964.

but, once made, it became impossible to read Reimarus, Strauss, Wrede and the others without seeing wishful thinking on every page.[19]

Schweitzer did not go on to provide a full-scale alternative account of Jesus. He simply offered what he called 'a sketch'. Schweitzer's Jesus was not a charming teacher of timeless wisdom; he was an 'apocalyptic Jewish prophet' (and self-proclaimed Messiah) who announced the end of the world and believed he was destined to suffer for his people to save them from the coming apocalypse.

Schweitzer's analysis was historically compelling. And no one could accuse him of projecting his own ideals on to Jesus; in fact, for decades after him scholars wondered whether the Jesus he had described had any relevance to the modern world. As Schweitzer himself noted, he had made Jesus 'a stranger and an enigma'.[20]

Almost single-handedly, then, Albert Schweitzer unravelled the quest for the historical Jesus. Not only had he 'erected its memorial', wrote a scholar of the next generation; he had 'delivered its funeral oration.'[21] If Enlightenment scholarship had undermined the church's simple faith in Jesus, Schweitzer's work brought to an end the Enlightenment's pretensions to rational objectivity. It would be half a century before anyone would revive the quest for the historical Jesus, and it would take an entirely new paradigm to get it going.

2

CHAPTER

The Quest for Jesus in the Twentieth Century and Beyond

Years of silence

After Albert Schweitzer there was almost half a century of conspicuous silence on the subject of the historical Jesus. Between 1906 and 1953 the topic received very little attention in academic circles. The Enlightenment confidence on the matter had been crushed, and no one quite knew what to do with Schweitzer's 'apocalyptic Jewish prophet'.

Rudolf Bultmann (1884–1976)

Theologians during this period of hiatus tended to approach the Gospels in an ahistorical way, almost as if the events of 5 BC–AD 30 were peripheral to Christian faith and life. The only solid detail was Jesus' death. No one doubted that. And for theological giants like Rudolf Bultmann the cross was just about all that mattered for theology. Jesus' birth and healings, and even his teachings, were considered inconsequential for modern faith.

Rudolf Bultmann
(1884–1976),
German theologian.

For Bultmann, the really important thing about the Jesus story is that behind the 'mythical garb' lies a divine call to an *existential decision*: to say 'yes' to God.[1] If that sounds a little esoteric, we should remember that the 1920s–40s were the high point of the philosophy of Existentialism. Existentialism stood in opposition to purely rationalistic forms of philosophy and science and emphasized that men and women exist in the moment. Therefore, what counts above everything else is that we choose in this moment to live authentically. Christian existentialism downplayed doctrine and history and stressed the need for the individual to choose God, the ultimate authenticator of life. Looking back on this retreat from history, the German scholar Günther Bornkam opened his 1956 volume by lamenting that 'scholarly treatments of Jesus of Nazareth, his message and history, have become, at least in Germany, increasingly rare'. He then added the wry observation: 'In their place there have appeared the numerous efforts of theologians turned poets and poets turned theologians.'[2]

The Second Quest: the twentieth-century recovery

It was only a matter of time, though, before the pendulum began to swing back (slowly) to a renewed appreciation of historical questions about Jesus. And it was one of Bultmann's most famous students who got the ball rolling again.

The 'New Quest' of Ernst Käsemann (1906–1998)

In 1953 Ernst Käsemann, a professor in Göttingen (moving later to Tübingen), gave a lecture titled 'The Problem of the Historical Jesus', in which he raised a question which over the last fifty years has received an increasingly positive answer. Does the church's image of the crucified and risen Saviour find any solid connection with what we know of the earthly man from Nazareth? Put another way, how

much of Christianity's post-Easter faith is supported by the Gospels' pre-Easter story? It was a modest question, but one that signalled the rise of a more measured and productive approach to the question of Jesus.[3]

The movement inspired by Käsemann is often called the 'New Quest' or 'Second Quest' for Jesus. It includes such significant names as Günther Bornkam, Ernst Fuchs and Norman Perrin.[4] Following Käsemann, these scholars devised rigorous tests for working out what was 'historical' in the Gospels and what was not. One such test, called the 'criterion of dissimilarity', highlights something of the character and limitations of this new quest.

The *criterion of dissimilarity* states that material in the Gospels which is markedly different from both Judaism and the early church is likely to have come from Jesus himself. The logic is as follows: teachings of Jesus with strong parallels in Judaism might, so it was thought, be the result of the Gospel writers trying to make Jesus fit with the Jewish culture of their day; and teachings of Jesus with strong parallels in early Christian practice might be attempts to justify later ecclesiastical traditions by having Jesus say it first.

Town view of Tübingen, Germany, home of Ernst Käsemann.

A Hasidic Jew casts a shadow on the Western Wall in Jerusalem, Israel.

So, in the midst of uncertainty, things that are doubly dissimilar (from Judaism and from Christianity) can be said with confidence to come from Jesus.

More recent scholars have criticized this particular test for historicity (while still endorsing a version of it). For one thing, suggesting that something is authentic because it was *not* picked up by the early church assumes that Jesus had little lasting impact on his followers. This is plainly ridiculous. Author after author in the New Testament affirms Jesus as the foundation of the Christian life.[5] Just as strangely, the suggestion that strongly Jewish themes cannot confidently be attributed to Jesus ignores one of the most obvious details of his life. He was a Jew living in Jewish Palestine. How could the historical Jesus *not* have sounded Jewish! The harshest criticism of this approach comes from the pen of the great Jewish scholar Professor Geza Vermes of Oxford University, who sees shades of anti-Semitism in the methodology: 'How, then, can anyone imagine that a saying of Jesus, in order to be authentic, had to distance itself from every known expression of "Jewish morality and piety"? Such an angle of approach is quite close to the old-fashioned anti-Semitic attitude according to which the aim of Jesus was to condemn and reject the whole Jewish religion.'[6]

There are some scholars operating today in the mode of the Second Quest. The so-called Jesus Seminar is a group of mainly American scholars led by Robert Funk. Members of the Seminar continue to apply the criterion of dissimilarity and other tests, and then vote on whether a certain saying or deed of Jesus is authentic (they literally get together and take votes). The result is a conglomerate of the Gospels published for the popular market in 1993, complete with colour-coding: black text for the parts that definitely did not come from Jesus, grey for those that probably did not, pink for the things that may correspond to something he said and red lettering for 'the authentic words of Jesus'. Needless to say, very little red ink was required in the printing.[7]

In a manner that few mainstream scholars would accept, the Seminar also emphasizes alternative Gospels, particularly the Gnostic Gospel of Thomas. In these Gnostic Gospels, which we will explore in Chapter 4, Jesus is stripped of his Jewish identity and his preaching is stripped of a future kingdom; he appears instead as a simple teacher of universal wisdom. Unsurprisingly, the Jesus that emerges from the Jesus Seminar is un-Jewish, uninterested in a future kingdom, and a perfect model of democracy, equality and freedom. He very much resembles the neo-liberal Christian academics who have devised him! The Jesus Seminar should be haunted by Albert Schweitzer's critique of nineteenth-century versions of Jesus – 'a figure designed by rationalism, endowed with life by liberalism, and clothed by modern theology in an historical garb' – but it isn't. 'Jesus has once again been modernized,' writes Professor James Dunn of Durham University, reflecting on the efforts of the Jesus Seminar, 'or should we rather say, post-modernized!'[8]

The Third Quest: significant advances in contemporary scholarship

Most scholars today are deeply sceptical about the methods and conclusions of the Second Quest just described. Divorcing Jesus from his first-century Jewish context amounts to a serious historical blunder, akin to trying to assess the life of Napoleon Bonaparte while ignoring eighteenth-century European philosophy and politics. In recognition of this deficiency many scholars have called for a new quest, a so-called Third Quest (following on from the flawed quests of the Enlightenment and the mid-twentieth-century).

Over the last thirty years a massive industry of academic literature has sprung up around the figure of Jesus. It does not all speak with one voice, but there is a wide consensus on at least one significant thing. The surest first step towards discovering the historical reality about the man from Nazareth is to locate him firmly in his first-century Palestinian environment.[9] The publication of the Dead Sea Scrolls – first found in 1947 but widely accessible only in the 1980s and 90s – has aided this effort to see Jesus in his Jewish context. The Scrolls have deepened and widened our picture of Judaism in a way that was impossible before.

The author interviewing Professor Martin Hengel.

Much of the rest of this book will reflect this most recent quest for the historical Jesus, so I will not labour the account here. Just three scholars deserve special mention at this point.

Martin Hengel (1926–2009)

Martin Hengel was Professor of New Testament and Ancient Judaism at Germany's prestigious University of Tübingen from 1972 (until his death, he was still there as Professor Emeritus, occasionally serving coffee and Brezel to admiring Australian scholars).[10]

An aerial view of Mount Masada, the site of Herod the Great's fortress. It was here that of one of the most famous battles between Jews and Romans took place. It ended in mass suicide in AD 73.

In some ways, Hengel was part of the mid-twentieth-century quest launched by Ernst Käsemann. This quest, as noted, applied a rigorous historical method to the task of uncovering the connections between the Jesus of history and the Christ of Christian faith. There is a significant difference, however. Whereas others in the so-called Second Quest downplayed the connections between Jesus and Judaism, and still others sought to play up the connections between Jesus and pagan religion, Hengel set out to clarify our picture of first-century Palestine and then to set Jesus and the Gospels within that secure context. He wrote a landmark account of the rise of Jewish revolutionaries in the first century (known as the Zealots),[11] and in his *Judaism and Hellenism* he helped to clarify the relationship between first-century Judaism and the broader Greek-speaking environment.[12]

Hengel also wrote works directly on the topic of Jesus. In *The Charismatic Leader and His Followers* he refuted the suggestion of theologians like Rudolf Bultmann that the early-church proclamation of Christ had little to do with the historical ministry of Jesus of Nazareth.[13] In *The Son of God* he challenged the once popular notion that Christian beliefs about a 'divine son' derived from pagan myths. He showed that the New Testament descriptions of Jesus derived from Jewish traditions (not pagan ones) current in Jerusalem in the period of Jesus himself.[14]

Ed Parish Sanders (born 1937)

Another key figure in the Third Quest is Professor Ed Sanders of Oxford University in the UK and then Duke University in the US. Like Hengel, Sanders is an expert in first-century Judaism. His book *Judaism: Practice and Belief, 63 BCE–66 CE*, remains a standard work on the subject.[15] He has applied this background to thorough analyses of both Jesus and the apostle Paul.

While Sanders' work on Paul has a great many detractors, his *Jesus and Judaism*, published in 1985, is still a seminal text in the field.[16] In this book Sanders shows how the Gospels' portrait of Jesus fits very plausibly into what we know of various movements in Judaism in the period before AD 70 (what is known as Second Temple Judaism). In particular, Sanders places Jesus within a movement in Judaism which longed for a new temple and a new age of God's presence in the world. This hope for a renewed Israel drove Jesus into conflict with the existing Temple authorities in Jerusalem and ultimately led to his death.

Norton Thomas Wright (born 1948)

N. T. Wright must also be mentioned in connection with the rise of the Third Quest. Indeed, he is probably the scholar who coined the term back in 1988, when he wrote: 'While the so-called "New Quest" [i.e., the Second Quest] was still cautiously arguing about presuppositions and methods, producing lengthy histories of tradition out of which

Part of the scroll of Isaiah which was found in the caves at Qumran, Israel. It dates from the Seond Temple Era.

could be squeezed one or two more drops of authentic Jesus-material, a quite different movement was beginning in a variety of places and with no unified background or programme.' This movement was becoming so prominent, Wright added, 'that it is not fanciful to talk in terms of a "Third Quest"'.[17]

N. T. Wright, or Tom Wright as he is commonly known, is also the present Anglican bishop of Durham. He is one of the few senior churchmen today to play a significant role in the largely secular historical study of Jesus. In his 1992 *The New Testament and the People of God* Wright laid out his methodology.[18] At its core, of course, was an account of Judaism in the period of Jesus and, in particular, of the hopes of the Jewish people at the time. Many in Jesus' day, Wright argued, looked forward to the restoration of God's people (Israel) and the renewal of all creation. The ancient 'exodus', when God delivered his people from Egyptian slavery and

Period	Ideas	Key figures
Ancient Quest (AD 30–500)	Rigorous analysis of the Gospels in service of the Christian faith.	Luke Origen Eusebius
First Quest (1600–1906)	Rejection of church 'dogma' coupled with an overly confident application of rationalist scepticism, producing a 'Jesus' cast in the mould of Enlightenment ideals.	Hermann Reimarus David Strauss Albert Schweitzer
Second Quest (1953– and dwindling)	Modest attempt to find some connection between the pre-Easter Jesus and the post-Easter Christian faith. Application of the criterion of dissimilarity.	Rudolf Bultmann Ernst Käsemann Norman Perrin US Jesus Seminar
Third Quest (1970– and thriving)	Sophisticated attempt to provide a plausible portrait of Jesus against the backdrop of the wealth of new archaeological and literary information about Second Temple Judaism (i.e., Jewish culture before AD 70).	Martin Hengel Ed Sanders Tom Wright Ben Meyer Marcus Borg John Meier James Dunn James Charlesworth Richard Bauckham Geza Vermes Paula Fredriksen Sean Freyne Graham Stanton Gerd Theissen

brought them into the Promised Land, was soon to be re-enacted on a cosmic scale as God brings his people out of exile and into freedom. Wright developed this theme of a 'return from exile' four years later in his *Jesus and the Victory of God*.[19] There he cast Jesus as an eschatological prophet who proclaimed the redemption of the captives and assured his people through words and deeds that God was becoming King of the cosmos. Not everyone agrees with Wright that 'exodus' and 'return from exile' are keys that unlock the whole story, but his portrait of Jesus as a prophet of renewal (for Israel and the world) is part of the mainstream consensus today.

Other important scholars of the contemporary Third Quest include Ben F. Meyer, Marcus J. Borg, John P. Meier, James Charlesworth, Sean Freyne, Graham Stanton, Gerd Theissen, James Dunn and Richard Bauckham. These scholars differ on many things – it is not a univocal movement – but the influence of Hengel, Sanders and Wright, especially their emphasis on the *Jewishness* of Jesus, can be seen throughout. 'What distinguishes this "third quest of the historical Jesus"', writes Professor James Dunn of the University of Durham, 'is the conviction that any attempt to build up a historical picture of Jesus of Nazareth should and must begin from the fact that he was a first-century Jew operating in a first-century milieu.'[20]

Overconfidence never bodes well for scholarship, and experts must always remain open to new evidence, but there is little doubt that the search for the historical Jesus is today on its surest footing since Luke wrote: 'I myself have carefully investigated everything from the beginning' (Luke 1:3).

I have no pretensions in this book to be *contributing* to the Third Quest for Jesus, but I certainly intend to embody its ethos and methods. Let me close this chapter by directing your attention to the table opposite. The (perhaps overly) neat table summarizes 2,000 years of Jesus research.

3
CHAPTER

A Brief History Lesson

There is one clear lesson to be learned from the history of 'historical Jesus research'. If we want to avoid fashioning Jesus into our own image, we must let our imaginations, preferences and dogmas bow before the available historical sources. The following chapters explore those sources. But first, let me say something about how to read history.

The accidents of history

Imagine, a thousand years from now, an archaeological team trying to piece together what life was like in your neighbourhood, with nothing to go on but a few random remains: the foundations of twenty houses, the ruin of a gym, thirty local newspapers (over a twenty-year period), a couple of hundred shopping receipts, a piggybank full of coins, some letters between lovers, and numerous unrelated household items including pictures, teapots, a fridge and some novels. On the basis of these there would be much that they could say about your stomping ground. From the house foundations they could work out the average size of a family and, from that, the population of the region. From the newspapers they could discern some important events and probably also something of the social and political views of the district. From the coins they could say something about the system of government. From the letters, receipts and novels they could make judgments about

Ruins at Beth Shean, a monumental Greco-Roman city within the borders of Israel.

Text of the letter of Dionysius son of Zoilus

To Philon the chief guard from Dionysius son of Zoilus who acts as antigrapheus to the oikonomos [i.e., secretary to the treasurer] for the revenue of the regions around Theogonis. On the 18th of the present month of Phamenoth when already the lamps were burning and I was washing in the new bathhouse called Aristodemus' and was using a calabash bowl, I was dragged off by Philon, one of the soldiers ... he set upon me with others, whose names I know not, and struck me with punches and kicks to whatever part of my body was available. They dragged me from the bathhouse and led me to the gate in the vicinity of the Samothracian temple. When certain guards appeared, they handed me over to them. Since therefore I am bedridden, I ask [you] to order the arrest of Philon and fellows until my complaint is investigated.

Bust of Emperor Tiberius (ruled AD 14–37). It was during his reign that Jesus preached and died.

the use of language, the state of the economy and the nature of social relationships. All of this would be accurate, to a point, but the reality is that most of what life was really like in your neighbourhood would remain hidden from them, even from the most perceptive future expert.

This really is what it is like to study the ancient world. What has survived of the writings and buildings of, say, first-century Jerusalem, Rome or Athens would amount to the tiniest fraction of what was actually penned and constructed in the period – probably less than 1 per cent. This 'fortuitousness and fragmentariness of surviving sources', as Professor Martin Hengel put it, means that history is rather hit and miss.[1] The randomness of what remains (and what does not) guarantees that what we know about the past is accidental and lopsided. Let me offer an example.

By a chance discovery of some ancient Greek letters written on papyrus, we happen to know about the plight of a certain second-century BC tax official named Dionysius, son of Zoilus. One evening, while strolling home from a recently opened public bathhouse, poor old Dionysius was mugged by a certain Philon and friends (ironically, Philon means 'love, friendship'). In his letter, Dionysius describes his utter humiliation, and he implores the city guard (who also happens to be named Philon) to arrest the thugs and investigate the case.[2] It is a delightful, random portrait of life in ancient times. But contrast this intimate snapshot of a lowly

bureaucrat with the fact that we do not possess a single personal
letter from Emperor Tiberius, the man who ruled the Roman world
from AD 14 to 37. Such is the unpredictability of historical evidence.

Let me offer another example of the unpredictability of historical
evidence, this time one closely related to Jesus studies. In passing,
the Gospel of John mentions a public bath in Jerusalem featuring
five colonnades or rows of columns.

> *Now there is in Jerusalem near the Sheep Gate a pool, which in*
> *Aramaic is called Bethesda, and which is surrounded by five*
> *covered colonnades.*
> **John 5:2**

Archaeological digs throughout Jerusalem failed to discover
the pool. Some scholars, such as J. Marsh and N. Krieger, began
proposing that such geographical details in John's Gospel were

fictitious or symbolic: perhaps the five colonnades of Bethesda represent the first five books of the Old Testament (Marsh's hypothesis).[3]

Then, between 1957 and 1962, a series of archaeological investigations uncovered a pool in the very area described by John; and, yes, there were five colonnades, one on each of the four sides, and one across the middle, dividing the pool from west to east.[4] As Urban C. von Wahlde writes in his recent review of the topic: 'The discovery of the pools proved beyond a doubt that the description of this pool was not the creation of the Evangelist [John] but reflected accurate and detailed knowledge of Jerusalem, knowledge that is sufficiently detailed to now be an aid to archaeologists in understanding the site.'[5]

Commentators who had doubted such geographical details were making the fundamental mistake of supposing that absence of corroborating evidence was evidence of absence. Scholars are usually much more wary of such assumptions. Cambridge professor Graham Stanton puts it succinctly: 'As every student of ancient history is aware, it is an elementary error to suppose that the unmentioned [or undiscovered] did not exist.'[6] History is too random and fragmentary for us to make firm judgments about what did not exist.

Another example illustrates how easily this scholarly dictum is overlooked in popular discussions about Jesus. In a long feature article in the *Australian Rationalist*, Chris Gaffney sought to demonstrate, among other things, that the evidence for Jesus is very much lacking:

> *Given that there are no contemporary references to Jesus while he was supposedly alive, we may even doubt his existence. There is not one mention of him in the many missives that passed from Palestine to Rome.*[7]

The statement is misleading on a number of levels. By 'contemporary references' Gaffney means documents written during Jesus' public ministry (AD 28–30). The assumption here is that only evidence written on the spot should count as real evidence. This would pretty much debunk the entire historiographical enterprise in one fell swoop. If contemporaneous record were the test of historicity, we would have

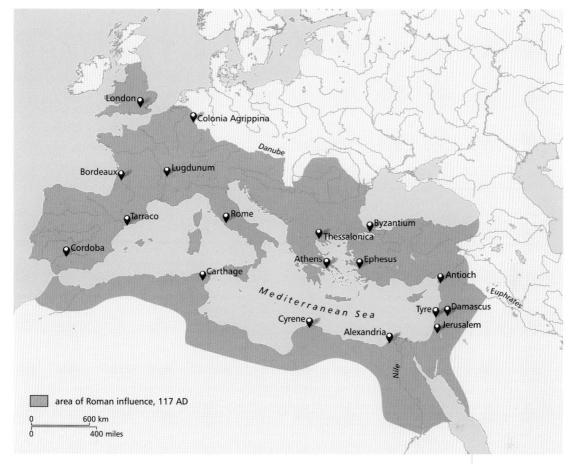

London
Colonia Agrippina
Danube
Bordeaux
Lugdunum
Tarraco
Rome
Byzantium
Thessalonica
Cordoba
Athens
Ephesus
Carthage
Antioch
Mediterranean Sea
Euphrates
Tyre
Damascus
Cyrene
Jerusalem
Alexandria
Nile

☐ area of Roman influence, 117 AD

0   600 km
0   400 miles

Map of the Roman empire, showing its areas of influence at the end of the first century AD.

to dismiss the existence of most of the people of the ancient world, including most kings, senators and generals, whom we generally only know about through accounts written *after the fact*.[8]

There is a more glaring mistake in Gaffney's remarks. No doubt there were 'many missives' between Palestine and Rome during the governorship of Pontius Pilate (AD 26–36) but, as I pointed out in my response to his article, if Gaffney has found one, there are thousands of historians waiting to read it! The reality is, *not one* such document has survived.[9] And even if we were to find some correspondence between Jerusalem and Rome during this period, it is not at all clear that we should expect to find mention of Jesus. He might be worshipped by millions today, but in AD 30 the Roman and Jerusalem authorities would have thought of him as a minor public nuisance.

It is true that writers roughly contemporaneous with Jesus are silent about the teacher from Nazareth. The Jewish philosopher Philo of Alexandria, for instance, lived from about 15 BC to AD 50. In his numerous volumes he says nothing about Jesus. Likewise, the first-century writer Justus of Tiberius wrote about Jewish kings and the Jewish war but fails to mention the Lord of the Christians. Are these silences significant? Probably not. Other figures whom we know lived in this period also failed to rate a mention in contemporary records. John the Baptist was a revered prophet figure in Palestine. He died shortly before Jesus. He is mentioned by the Jewish writer Josephus but not by Philo or any other Jewish rabbinic text. Again, Paul of Tarsus, the greatest of the early Christian missionaries, whose authentic letters we have in our possession, is mentioned by no non-Christian author. The Teacher of Righteousness was a revered leader of the Essene Jews at Qumran and is a central character in the Dead Sea Scrolls, yet none of the ancient reports about the Essenes (in Philo, Josephus, Pliny the Elder) mentions him. Perhaps most surprising is the fact that Rabbi Hillel, the greatest of the Jewish teachers in the tradition of the Pharisees, is never mentioned by Josephus, who was himself a Pharisee. The point of all this is to say that the absence of Jesus from some ancient writings is no more significant than the absence of other important (and certain) figures from similar writings.[10] Such is the randomness of history.

The unpredictability of history and the relative anonymity of Jesus combine to lower most scholars' expectations about the kind of evidence we should hope to find concerning him. But as it turns out, the randomness of history has worked in our favour in this case. The data assessed by scholars of the historical Jesus is rather plentiful.

Introducing the sources

First, there are the so-called Gnostic Gospels and related literature, discussed in the next chapter. These texts have received enormous popular attention in recent years, partly because of their potentially explosive content. They provide alternative pictures of Jesus, ones that challenge traditional Christian dogma. Readers will soon learn, however, that for all the popular interest in these writings, modern

Fragment of the Gospel of Thomas from the Nag Hammadi codices which were discovered in 1945.

scholars consider them only marginally useful for understanding the life of Jesus. For one thing, they are the latest of the works in our catalogue of 'evidence' for Jesus. The time frame matters to historians. Though it is unreasonable to insist on contemporaneous records, the further away a text is from the events it recounts, the less likely it is to retain reliable information. We begin our search for reliable information about Jesus with these second- and third-century works, but, like an investigator on the trail of a discovery, our aim is to move closer and closer to earlier, more credible information about our subject. We will arrive at one small piece of evidence that can be dated to within months of Jesus' death.

After the Gnostic Gospels we examine the Greco-Roman and Jewish writings which refer to Jesus (Chapters 5–6). Not all of these are of great value, but several are taken very seriously by contemporary experts. There is a lot of popular nonsense written about these passages. In his *Atheist Manifesto* French philosopher Michel Onfray dismisses them all as wholesale 'ideological fabrication,' composed by ancient Christians to give their heavenly saviour an earthly existence.[11] Such spoiling arguments are not taken seriously by the experts. While it is important not to overstate the significance of non-Christian references to Jesus, several of the passages to be discussed do 'render highly implausible any far-fetched theories that even Jesus' very existence was a Christian invention', writes Christopher Tuckett, Professor of New Testament at the University of Oxford.[12]

Inevitably, in Chapters 7–8 we confront the question of the relative

value of the New Testament for understanding the historical Jesus. I realize I have an uphill battle here. The popular suspicion towards religion leads many to think that the New Testament should not be accorded even the status of an ordinary human record. Because God is a myth, so the logic goes, any text infused with a belief in God must, by definition, be mythical, not historical. However, the conviction that the world is divinely ordered permeates virtually all texts of the ancient world, whether Josephus, Tacitus or Pliny, but this does not mean the events recounted in these texts are necessarily mythological. Contemporary scholars learn simply to ignore the background religious assumptions of ancient writers and examine their reports for their earthly, historical information. This is exactly how the secular study of Jesus proceeds, and it is what distinguishes the discipline of New Testament history, a sub-field of ancient history, from the discipline of Christian theology, which is a type of philosophy. In this book there will be no theology (as valuable as that field is), only history. The methods historians use to sort out fact from fiction in the story of Jesus will be the subject of Chapters 9–10.

When all of these sources are examined – from the second-century Gnostic Gospel of Thomas to the earliest text of the New Testament – a plausible picture of Jesus does slowly emerge. Despite

Modern-day view across Lake Galilee.

the protestations of the professional nay-sayers, there has emerged over the last twenty years a broad consensus about the figure at the heart of the Christian faith. Some details of his life are regarded as historically certain. Professor Ed Sanders of Duke University is one of the leading figures of the Third Quest for Jesus and no propagandist for the Christian religion. In his *The Historical Figure of Jesus* he listed the details which can be regarded as *established* by historical method:

> *I shall first offer a list of statements about Jesus that meet two standards: they are almost beyond dispute; and they belong to the framework of his life, and especially of his public career: Jesus was born c. 4 BCE, near the time of the death of Herod the Great; he spent his childhood and early adult years in Nazareth, a Galilean village; he was baptized by John the Baptist; he called disciples; he taught in the towns, villages and countryside of Galilee (apparently not the cities); he preached 'the kingdom of God'; about the year 30 he went to Jerusalem for Passover; he created a disturbance in the Temple area; he had a final meal with the disciples; he was arrested and interrogated by Jewish authorities, specifically the high priest; he was executed on the orders of the Roman prefect, Pontius Pilate. We may add here a short list of equally secure facts about the aftermath of Jesus' life: his disciples fled; they saw him (in what sense is not certain) after his death; as a consequence, they believed that he would return to found the kingdom; they formed a community to await his return and sought to win others to faith in him as God's Messiah.*[13]

I have explored these details in a systematic way in my *Jesus: A Short Life*. The present book is really an account of the sources and methods used by scholars such as Sanders (and thousands more like him) to arrive at their conclusions about the biography of Jesus. *Investigating Jesus* is about *how* we know what we know.

CHAPTER

The Gnostic Gospels

Best-selling novelist Dan Brown is to be congratulated for bringing to popular attention a group of texts which scholars have been working on for decades but which, until the publication of *The Da Vinci Code*, they had simply assumed would be of little interest to the general public. Let me remind readers of the centrally important scene in Brown's classic 2003 novel, in which scholar Sir Leigh Teabing explains to Sophie Neveu, the French cryptologist, that most of what she thought was true about Jesus probably was not. It all has to do with which Gospels you turn to:

> *'Jesus Christ was a historical figure of staggering influence, perhaps the most enigmatic and inspirational leader the world has ever seen ... Understandably, His life was recorded by thousands of followers across the land.' Teabing paused to sip his tea and then placed the cup back on the mantel. 'More than eighty gospels were considered for the New Testament, and yet only a relative few were chosen for inclusion – Matthew, Mark, Luke and John among them.'*
>
> *'Who chose which gospels to include?' Sophie asked.*
>
> *'Aha!' Teabing burst in with enthusiasm. 'The fundamental irony of Christianity! The Bible, as we know it today, was collated by the pagan Roman emperor Constantine the Great.'*
>
> *'Constantine commissioned and financed a new Bible, which omitted those gospels that spoke of Christ's human traits and*

embellished those gospels that made Him godlike. The earlier gospels were outlawed, gathered up, and burned …'

'Fortunately for historians,' Teabing said, 'some of the gospels that Constantine attempted to eradicate managed to survive. The Dead Sea Scrolls were found in the 1950s hidden in a cave near Qumran in the Judaean desert. And, of course, the Coptic Scrolls in 1945 at Nag Hammadi. In addition to telling the true Grail story, these documents speak of Christ's ministry in very human terms. Of course, the Vatican, in keeping with their tradition of misinformation, tried very hard to suppress the release of these scrolls.'[1]

The scene has all the ingredients of a plausible conspiracy: abuse of great power, corruption in traditional institutions, and fortuitous discoveries. The plausibility was rehearsed more recently by Richard Dawkins, the former Professor for the Public Understanding of Science at Oxford University. 'The four Gospels that made it into the official canon', he writes, 'were chosen, more or less arbitrarily, out of a larger sample of at least a dozen including the Gospels of Thomas, Peter, Nicodemus, Philip, Bartholomew and Mary Magdalen.' He then adds: 'But there is no more and no less reason to believe the four canonical gospels. All have the status of legends,' he assures us. Dawkins is unaware of the overwhelming evidence, amassed by Professor Martin Hengel, that the four New Testament Gospels were a fixed, authoritative collection by at least the middle of the second century, before most of the Gnostics had even begun to put pen to papyrus (and also, by the way, long before Constantine was born).[2] Moreover, none of the Gnostic Gospels was ever even considered for inclusion in the New Testament. When the great church councils got together in the third and fourth centuries to discuss which books were part of the canon (which means 'rule, standard'), there was no argument about the Gospels. Their inclusion, along with the letters of the apostle Paul, had long been established.[3] Only with a fertile imagination can it be argued that the four New Testament Gospels were chosen 'arbitrarily' out of a larger sample of alternative Gospels. This will become clearer as we

Marble bust of the first Christian emperor, Constantine (ruled AD 307–337).

explore what modern scholars are saying about the discovery and significance of the Gnostic writings.

A discovery in Egypt

In 1945 a collection of manuscripts was uncovered in the Egyptian town of Nag Hammadi, 500 km south of Cairo. The thirteen codices (or books) were found in a storage jar buried underneath a boulder. Bizarrely, the man who made the discovery, whose name was Muhammad Ali, took the priceless documents back to his home, where his mother burned some of the pages as fuel for her bread oven. Fortunately, they were soon viewed by antiquities dealers and made available for scholarly assessment.

We have no firm information about who originally owned the books or about why they were hidden in this way sometime in the fourth century. Some have speculated that the collection was being protected from an inquisitorial Vatican eager to stamp out

Loose fragments of papyrus from the Gnostic text of the Gospel of Judas are assembled by Florence Darbre and Gregor Wurst in Darbre's conservation lab in Geneva, Switzerland in 2007.

The Coptic Museum of Cairo, Egypt, houses the world's largest collection of Coptic Christian artefacts, including the Nag Hammadi Codices.

alternative Gospels, but there is nothing to indicate this and it is just as likely that the leather-bound books – a precious commodity in antiquity – were being hidden from thieves, invaders or just the elements.

After years of wrangling between collectors and museums, the thirteen codices are now kept in the beautiful Coptic Museum of Cairo. I was shocked when I visited the museum recently to discover that, apart from the few pages beautifully displayed for the public, these precious volumes are stored in a dusty back room with no climate control. As the curator reached into what looked like a huge grandfather cabinet to pull out the Gospels of Thomas and Philip, a small fragment of one page slipped out of position and into the corner of the Perspex cover. I was the only one who looked alarmed.

Who were the Gnostics?

Within these thirteen volumes are a total of fifty-two separate works, many of which betray a clear Gnostic influence. From the Greek word for knowledge (*gnosis*), 'Gnosticism' was a philosophical movement of the second and third centuries. It had roots in Judaism, Greek ideas and even Persian (Iranian) thought. In its Christian form it insisted that the traditional Jesus story needed to be reworked with special information the Lord had secretly revealed to a select few during his lifetime: to Thomas in the Gospel of Thomas, to Philip in the Gospel of Philip, and so on.

The heart of the Gnostic secret was as follows. Although our human spirits are of divine origin, they are sadly trapped in this corrupt material world. This world was created by a lesser deity known as the Demiurge ('craftsman'), who is also identified with the God of the Jews. He is not the supreme divinity, according to the Gnostic view. Thus, escape from the physical realm into the 'kingdom of light' comes not through devotion to the Demiurge, the Creator God of the Jews, but through knowledge of the 'Highest Being', who is the source of the divine spark within us. Jesus came from this being to offer us correct knowledge.[4]

It is clear that the Gnostic Gospels are not an independent collection of writings equal in age and value to the New Testament Gospels. They are instead a *reaction* to the Jewish traditions about Jesus already found in the New Testament. 'Their mythology consisted of an "exegetical protest" against the older and widely accepted traditions,' writes Professor Dr Dr Kurt Rudolph (his real titles) in his review of scholarship on the Gnostic Gospels. 'This involved a reinterpretation of the older traditions in a manner which was opposed to their original sense.'[5] In other words, the Gnostic Gospels were an exercise in ancient revisionism, an attempt to recast the originally Jewish Jesus into a form more acceptable to the anti-Jewish, anti-creation perspectives of Gnosticism.

The Gospel of Judas

This revisionism is blatant in the Gnostic text that caught the world's attention in the 2006 National Geographic documentary, *The Gospel of Judas* (2006). Here it was announced to the world that a document

In Washington, USA, a panel, part of the the exhibit of the Gospel of Judas, is on display at the National Geographic headquarters. The panel shows what the codex containing the gospel looked like before conservation work was begun. The ancient manuscript dates from the third or fourth century AD and it is the only known surviving copy of the Gospel of Judas. The text portrays Judas as acting at Jesus' request when he hands Jesus over to the authorities.

had been uncovered, again in Egypt, which purports to be from the traditional betrayer of Jesus himself. According to the text, the real hero of the story was Judas; the eleven other apostles simply got Jesus wrong. The film-makers constantly used the word 'authentic', but did not make it sufficiently clear to viewers that this did not mean that the document was actually written by Judas (no one is arguing that); rather, it means that the fourth-century manuscript at the centre of the documentary is not a modern forgery but a true copy of a second-century work known as the Gospel of Judas.[6] Before the discovery of this manuscript in the 1970s we knew of the Gospel of Judas only through a passing criticism of it by the late second-century Christian writer Bishop Irenaeus of Lyons (AD 180).

Media sensationalism aside, the Gospel of Judas provides a transparent example of the Gnostics' attempt to rewrite the history of Jesus to fit with their own developing system of thought. The document begins: 'The secret account of the revelation that Jesus spoke in conversation with Judas Iscariot during a week three days before he celebrated Passover.'[7] The core claim of this Gospel is that the eleven other apostles were deluded and worshipped a lesser deity they presumed to be the true God. Jesus, however, took Judas aside and revealed to him the truth about the myriad spiritual realities over which he (Judas), as the leader of true Christianity, would one day rule. Jesus is quite explicit: no one from the generation of the eleven apostles had true *gnosis*. Judas is the great priest who sacrifices the body of Jesus and so is elevated to celestial, if not historical, glory. A key passage has Jesus – that is, the Gnostic narrator – discounting the eleven apostles, insisting that Judas alone has received the truth:

One day he was with his disciples in Judea, and he found them gathered together and seated in pious observance. When he [approached] his disciples, gathered together and seated and offering a prayer of thanksgiving over the bread, [he] laughed. The disciples said to [him], 'Master, why are you laughing at [our] prayer of thanksgiving? We have done what is right.'

He answered and said to them, 'I am not laughing at you. [You] are not doing this because of your own will but because it is through this that your god [will be] praised.'

They said, 'Master, you are […] the son of our god.'

Jesus said to them, 'How do you know me? Truly [I] say to you, no generation of the people that are among you will know me.'

When his disciples heard this, they started getting angry and infuriated and began blaspheming against him in their hearts. When Jesus observed their lack of [understanding, he said] to them, 'Why has this agitation led you to anger? Your god who is within you and […] have provoked you to anger [within] your souls. [Let] any one of you who is [strong enough] among human beings bring out the perfect human and stand before my face.'

They all said, 'We have the strength.' But their spirits did not dare to stand before [him], except for Judas Iscariot. He was able to stand before him, but he could not look him in the eyes, and he turned his face away.

Judas [said] to him, 'I know who you are and where you have come from. You are from the immortal realm of Barbelo [an emanation of highest being]. And I am not worthy to utter the name of the one who has sent you.'

Knowing that Judas was reflecting upon something that was exalted, Jesus said to him, 'Step away from the others and I shall tell you the mysteries of the kingdom. It is possible for you to reach it, but you will grieve a great deal. For someone else will replace you, in order that the twelve [disciples] may again come to completion with their god [i.e., the false God of creation].'

Gospel of Judas 33–36

Jesus being betrayed by Judas's kiss is depicted in this late fifteenth-century painting by Jean Bourdichon, *The Kiss of Judas*.

Keeping in mind that this text was composed around the middle of the second century, more than a century after the real Judas, the narrator's strategy is plain. The 'truth' was granted not to the mainstream apostles and those who follow their teaching, but to Judas, whose insights are preserved only in the group which produced the Gospel in his name. In other words, mainstream Christianity of the second century, with its strong Jewish heritage and devotion to the God of creation, is simply wrong, according to the Gospel of Judas.

A fragment of the Gospel of Philip. It is housed in the Coptic Museum of Cairo.

The Gospel of Philip and the kiss

A similar strategy is found in the Gospel of Philip, a text probably composed shortly after the Gospel of Judas.[8] It too insists that true knowledge is not to be found in a straightforward understanding of core Christian teachings about God, Jesus, the Holy Spirit, the resurrection or the church. When thought of in an earthly way, these words 'are the cause of a great deception', says verse 11. Rather, true knowledge is found in the ineffable secrets of the higher realm which this Gospel discloses. But perhaps the Gospel of Philip's greatest claim to fame is its purported reference to Jesus' wife:

> [Saying] No. 55. The S[aviour lov]ed [Ma]ry Mag[da]lene more than [all] the disciples, and kissed on her [mouth] often. The other [disciples] ... [ ]. They said to him: 'Why do you love her more than all of us?' The Saviour answered and said to them [ ]: 'Why do I not love you like her?'[9]

The bracketed sections in this quotation indicate the parts of the original manuscript, written in Coptic, which cannot be read, because of either fading or tearing of the papyrus. 'Mouth' is

The author with fragments of the Gospel of Thomas.

actually a guess. That did not stop Dan Brown in *The Da Vinci Code* making as much as he could of the passage, declaring that Jesus' marriage to Mary was 'a matter of historical record'.[10] What readers of the novel did not know is that the writer of the Gospel of Philip almost certainly never meant to imply anything romantic in this encounter. If, as Gnostic expert Professor Peter Nagel says, 'Gnostic ethics is marked by hostility to the body and striving to escape from the world',[11] a love story was probably the last thing on the ancient author's mind. The kiss was nothing more than a religious act, for we know that the 'ritual kiss' was a common practice of Gnostic sects. Also, the fact that the male apostles in this scene are jealous of Jesus' love for Mary should make it obvious that this gesture is spiritual, not romantic. And a larger point must not be overlooked. The Gospel of Philip was written so long after Mary, Jesus and Philip lived that most scholars find it difficult to believe it contains any independent historical information. It tells us quite a bit about Christian splinter groups in the second century, but nothing about the teacher who lived and died more than 130 years earlier.

Authentic sayings in the Gospel of Thomas?

This is not to say that Gnostic literature contains nothing of value. Many scholars agree that one Gnostic text probably does contain a handful of authentic sayings of the historical Jesus. The Gospel of Thomas appears immediately before the Gospel of Philip in Codex 2 of the Nag Hammadi manuscripts. Its opening statement shares the same general outlook as other Gnostic writings: 'These are the secret words which the living Jesus spoke, and which Didymus Judas Thomas wrote down. And he said: He who shall find the interpretation of these words shall not taste of death.'[12] The bulk of the 114 'secret words' in this text have no real claim to be the actual words of the teacher from Nazareth.

The Gospel of Thomas is generally believed to be the earliest of the Gnostic writings. The standard English edition of these writings states: 'There is much in favour of the view that [the Gospel of] Thomas originated about the middle of the 2nd century in Eastern Syria, although admittedly the collected sayings material may in part go back even into the 1st century.'[13] This relatively early date,

Did Jesus marry?

It has been suggested that pious first-century Jews were obliged to get married. Without evidence to the contrary, so the argument runs, we should assume that Jesus had a wife. Dan Brown's fictional scholar Robert Langdon puts it forcefully: 'The social decorum during that time virtually forbade a Jewish man to be unmarried. According to Jewish custom, celibacy was condemned.'[1] How true is this?

Marriage was highly regarded among ancient Jews. In fact, this is one of the reasons non-fictional scholars are pretty sure Jesus did not have a wife. If he did marry, the Gospel writers – who mentioned a dozen other relatives of Jesus – are sure to have mentioned it, since they all honoured marriage. That said, despite the high value placed on matrimony by ancient Jews, it is simply false to say that celibacy was forbidden or condemned. Some pious Jews we know of gave up the gift of marriage in order to perform special services to God. Even in the Old Testament the prophet Jeremiah abstained from the blessing of marriage as a sign of Israel's doom.[2] Some of the Essene Jews, who gave us the Dead Sea Scrolls and were roughly contemporary to Jesus, advocated celibacy as a mark of devotion.[3] Another group of celibate Jews, known as the Therapeutae, lived in Alexandria (Egypt) in the first century – there were male and female members of this movement.[4] The point is: an unmarried Jewish teacher in this period would have been viewed not as scandalous but as unusually devout.

We do not know why Jesus might have chosen celibacy: perhaps it was a sign to Israel, on the model of the ancient prophet Jeremiah; perhaps he wanted to remain focused on his gruelling preaching and travelling ministry; perhaps he simply wanted to save any potential beloved from the grief associated with his controversial and ultimately dangerous career path. What we can say with confidence is that Jesus was not against marriage. His words on the theme make this clear, as does the fact that his apostles and relatives were married (they even took their wives with them on missionary tours).[5]

compared to the other Gnostic writings, encourages many scholars to accept that some of the sayings may indeed come from Jesus, particularly those which sound rather *un*like Gnosticism and quite like the earlier Gospels (those now in the New Testament). First, there are statements which appear to be deliberate reworkings of material in the New Testament Gospels. For instance, in Mark 12:17 Jesus is reported to have said: 'Give to Caesar what is Caesar's and to God what is God's.' In the Gospel of Thomas this saying becomes: 'What belongs to Caesar, give to Caesar; what belongs to God, give to God; and what is mine, give it to me.' The words 'and what is mine, give it to me' may *possibly* be authentic, but it is more likely they have been added to the original saying for the sake of 'theological completeness'.

There are other sayings in the Gospel of Thomas which many believe do come from the historical Jesus and are not simple reworkings of material in the canonical or New Testament Gospels. The following five are the strongest candidates:

No. 42. Jesus said: Become passers-by.

No. 81. Jesus said: He who has become rich, let him become king, and he who has power, let him renounce it.

No. 82. Jesus said: He who is near to me is near the fire, and he who is far from me is far from the kingdom.

No. 97. Jesus said: The kingdom of the Father is like a woman carrying a jar full of meal. While she was walking on a distant road, the handle of the jar broke and the meal poured out behind her on the road. She was unaware, she had not noticed the misfortune. When she came to her house, she put the jar down and found it empty.

No. 98. Jesus said: The kingdom of the Father is like a man who wanted to kill a powerful man. He drew the sword in his house and drove it into the wall, that he might know that his hand would be strong enough. Then he slew the powerful man.

There is no way to be sure that these statements come from Jesus himself. However, we do know that 'oral tradition', the memorization and rehearsal of Jesus' words and deeds, was still an important part of church life in the early second century. This means it is entirely plausible that some 'stray' teachings of Jesus were kept alive *verbally* for a century before being written down. I will say more about oral tradition at a later point. Suffice it to say now that in the ancient world oral tradition was frequently a more trusted – and more trustworthy – method of preserving cultural memories than written records which only an elite few could access and read. While some scholars doubt that Thomas has preserved any independent information about Jesus, many think otherwise. The fact that the above five sayings contain no hint of Gnosticism (which would indicate a second-century origin) and strongly resonate with what we find in our canonical Gospels inspires

Some inauthentic sayings from the Gospel of Thomas

No. 29. Jesus said: If the flesh came into existence because of the spirit, it is a marvel. But if the spirit came into existence because of the body, it is a marvel of marvels. But as for me, I wonder at this, how this great wealth made its home in this poverty.

No. 50. Jesus said: If they say to you: Whence have you come?, say to them: We have come from the light, the place where the light came into being of itself. It established itself, and it revealed itself in their image.

No. 77. Jesus said: I am the light that is above them all. I am the all; the all came forth from me, and the all attained to me. Cleave a piece of wood, I am there. Raise up a stone, and you will find me there.

No. 108. Jesus said: He who drinks from my mouth will become like me, and I will become like him, and the hidden things will be revealed to him.

No. 114. Simon Peter said to them: Let Mariham go out from among us, for women are not worthy of the life. Jesus said: Look, I will lead her that I may make her male, in order that she too may become a living spirit resembling you males. For every woman who makes herself male will enter into the kingdom of heaven.

At one point, the Gnostic rejection of the (original) Jewish Jesus is apparent in Thomas. Jewish tradition held that the number of prophets who addressed Israel in the holy Scriptures was twenty-four.[1] With this in mind a reported dialogue between Jesus and the disciples in the Gospel of Thomas is telling:

No. 52. His disciples said to him: Twenty-four prophets spoke in Israel, and they all spoke of you. He said to them: You have abandoned the living one before your eyes, and spoken about the dead.

The message is potent: to think of Jesus as the fulfilment of the Scriptures of Israel is to associate the 'living one' with a bunch of dead men. This is a clear critique of the perspective of the first Christians.

confidence that this Gospel, alone of all the Gnostics, has retained at least a few authentic statements of Jesus.

The value of the Gnostic writings

In terms of our search for reliable sources for Jesus, even the

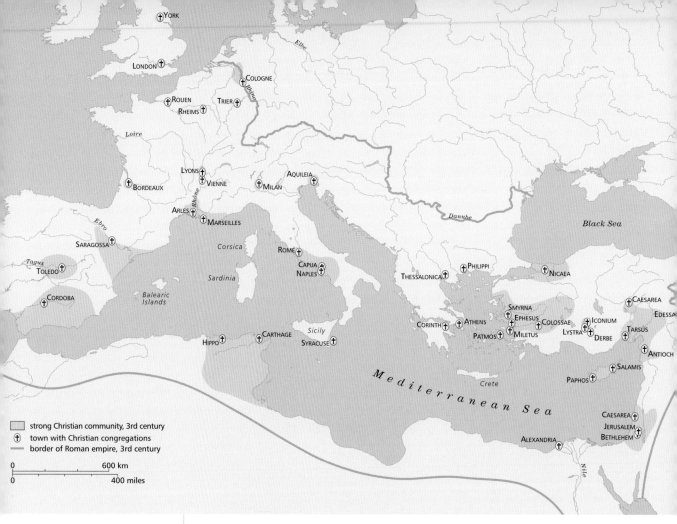

Map showing the spread of Christianity up to the third century AD.

Gospel of Thomas – the only Gnostic text widely believed to contain authentic material from Jesus – does not prove as useful as we might have hoped. 'While the historian must always be grateful for new scraps of evidence,' writes Professor Graham Stanton in his textbook on Jesus, 'these five sayings [in Thomas] hardly mark a dramatic advance.'[14] In fact, no new theme in Jesus' teaching is found in these 'scraps', and certainly no new historical information about him can be uncovered.

So, what is the significance of the Gnostic Gospels? While a few scholars continue to argue that one or two of the Gnostic texts ought to be given equal weight to the New Testament Gospels,[15] this remains a minority view with little sign of growth. The main value of the Gnostic Gospels is to reveal how diverse second- and third-century Christianity was. Gone are the days when we thought of the early church as a monochrome movement. Variety appeared quite early on in its history. There is no way to tell whether the Gnostics were ever more than a small collection of splinter groups within Christianity, but they certainly had a life of their own, quite separate from other Christians (and in opposition to them). The Gospels of Thomas, Philip, Judas and the others are windows into the diversity. They tell us little about the man who taught in the first part of the first century, but a great deal about some of his admirers a century or two later.

After a lengthy discussion of the topic, leading US scholar, Professor John P. Meier of the University of Notre Dame, describes the frustrating situation confronting the historian in search of Jesus. For all the promise held out by the discovery of these additional Gospels, the evidence forces us back to the tiny pool of historical material found in the New Testament:

> *We are left alone – some would say forlorn – with the Four Gospels, plus scattered tidbits. It is only natural for scholars – to say nothing of popularizers – to want more, to want other access roads to the historical Jesus. This understandable but not always critical desire is, I think, what has recently led to the high evaluation, in some quarters, of the apocryphal gospels and the Nag Hammadi codices as sources for the quest. It is a case of the wish being father to the thought, but the wish is a pipe dream. For better or for worse, in our quest for the historical Jesus, we are largely confined to the canonical Gospels; the genuine 'corpus' is infuriating in its restrictions. For the historian it is a galling limitation. But to call upon the Gospel of Peter or the Gospel of Thomas to supplement our Four Gospels is to broaden out our pool of sources from the difficult to the incredible.[16]*

If our search for sources is looking grim, a few more 'scattered tidbits' of information about Jesus can be found in another group of writings from the first and second centuries. In the next two chapters we explore the references to Jesus in non-Christian sources.

5
CHAPTER

Non-Christian References to Jesus from the Second Century

In Chapter 3 we explored the frustrating randomness of historical evidence. Not only do we possess probably less than 1 per cent of the literary works of the relevant period, but what has survived is uneven and not necessarily representative. This makes the study of the ancient world both frustrating (because our knowledge is fragmentary) and exciting (because you never know what might turn up). It just so happens that, in the case of Jesus, the fortuitousness of history has worked in our favour. By a happy accident of history Jesus appears in passing in numerous passages of the first and second centuries. These are certainly not all of equal value, and in what follows I will make clear which texts provide good evidence for Jesus and which do not.

Talmud (second century): Jesus the sorcerer

The ancient Jewish legal book known as the Talmud contains one probable reference to Jesus as a magician and deceiver who was rightly executed for his crimes.[1] Although the Talmud was compiled

Let me alert readers to two mistakes people make when looking at these non-Christian references to Jesus.

For the keen believer the fact that Jesus is mentioned by unbelievers in the period could be interpreted as proof positive for Jesus and therefore as a basis for strengthened faith. In my view, this is asking too much, especially since, for the most part, the texts are brief, late and open to alternative interpretations.

But there is a second mistake people make when looking at these non-Christian texts, and it is equally wide of the mark. Some doggedly sceptical people – and a few academics among them – badly underestimate the significance of these references. Disinclined to accept any evidence in favour of Jesus, they insist that all such texts must be counterfeits. 'Nothing of what remains can be trusted,' declares French atheist Michel Onfray. 'Even the writings of Flavius Josephus, Suetonius, or Tacitus, who mention in a few hundred words the existence of Christ and his faithful in the first century of our era, obey the rules of intellectual forgery.'[1] Few experts today go along with Onfray, but some remain wary of the non-Christian references to Jesus on the grounds that they are mere responses to Christian claims and so do not represent *independent* testimony. This is an exaggeration of a partial truth. Non-Christian references to Jesus may well have been written *in reaction* to Christian claims, but this in no way empties them of their historical significance. The descriptions of Jesus found in these passages are very different from those in the Christian Gospels. This

tells us that, wherever these non-Christian writers got their information about Jesus, it was not from the New Testament itself. These texts therefore have to be treated as *independent* of the Gospels. In their acclaimed textbook on the historical Jesus, Professors Gerd Theissen and Annette Merz (University of Heidelberg) write:

The extra-Christian sources are probably a reaction to Christian statements. But one should not put their value as sources too low either. First, they go back to Christian statements which are probably independent of our Gospels. They are independent testimony. Secondly, they document the ambivalent attitude of both Jewish and pagan contemporaries ... Thirdly, they show that contemporaries in the first and second century saw no reason to doubt Jesus' existence.[2]

Avoiding both Christian apologetics and dogmatic scepticism, let me unpack the non-Christian references to Jesus in reverse chronological order.

A rabbi reads the Talmud, the ancient Jewish legal book.

into a single volume between the fifth and sixth centuries, the relevant passage below is widely believed to date from the second century:[2]

On the Sabbath of the Passover festival Jesus (Yeshu) the Nazarene was hanged [i.e., on a cross]. For forty days before execution took place, a herald went forth and cried: 'Here is Jesus the Nazarene, who is going forth to be stoned because he has practised sorcery and enticed Israel to apostasy. Anyone who can say anything in his favour, let him come forth and plead on his behalf.' But since nothing was brought forth in his favour, he was hanged on the eve of the Passover.
Talmud (baraitha Sanhedrin 43a)[3]

It has been argued that the words 'Jesus' and 'the Nazarene' did not appear in the original version of this passage but were added later. However, 'Jesus' appears in all of our Talmud manuscripts and is certainly original. The words *ha Notzri*, 'the Nazarene', on the other hand, appear in one manuscript only, the so-called Munich manuscript. When faced with this kind of discrepancy, scholars ask: Which is more likely: that the words were added to one manuscript or that they were removed from another? In this case, the scales lean slightly in favour of the accuracy of the Munich manuscript. Why? Because while it is easy to understand why 'the Nazarene' might have been omitted from some manuscripts (to avoid giving offence to Christians), it is difficult to understand why the reference would have been added. Jews were hardly going to stir up trouble with Christians by turning a vague slander about an unknown 'Jesus' into a precise blasphemy against Jesus of Nazareth, and Christians are even less likely to have done this. It also has to be remembered that, until the modern period, no one (not even sceptics) had thought to suggest that Jesus never lived. There was thus no plausible motivation for inventing 'proofs', especially ones so derogatory towards Jesus.[4]

Determined sceptics aside, 'it is universally agreed', writes Professor Robert E. Van Voorst of this passage in the recent *Encyclopedia of the Historical Jesus*, 'that the Jesus (Yeshu) here is Jesus of Nazareth'.[5]

The paragraph is slightly confused. Jesus was crucified ('hanged' is the Hebrew way of referring to crucifixion), but he was also stoned. This is almost certainly an attempt to make the treatment of Jesus accord with Jewish law, since the stipulated penalty for sorcery was stoning, not crucifixion. Similarly suspicious is the reference to the forty-day search for witnesses for the defendant. All scholars agree that this detail was added to the story to improve the appearance of legal procedure – this whole booklet, *baraitha Sanhedrin*, concerns proper legal method.

The historical core of the passage is the conviction and crucifixion near the time of the Passover of a sorcerer and deceiver named Jesus the Nazarene. Interestingly, a Christian writer of the early second century indirectly confirms this Jewish criticism. Justin Martyr, writing around AD 140, says that the Jews 'dared to call him a magician and a deceiver of the people'.[6] The connection with *baraitha Sanhedrin* is strong ('he has practised sorcery and enticed Israel to apostasy'). At least by the early second century it seems that the Jewish leadership was being forced to explain how and why the famous Jesus of Nazareth was put to death.

Bust of Emperor Nero, who ruled from AD 54–68. He executed Christians, including (probably) the apostles Peter and Paul.

Tacitus (AD 115): Jesus and his deadly superstition

Those of us who learned anything at school about Rome and its emperors – Tiberius, Caligula, Claudius, Nero and so on – have one man to thank, Cornelius Tacitus, without doubt the most important ancient source on first-century Rome. He mentions Jesus and his followers in passing and in a rather unflattering way.

Tacitus was born about AD 56. An aristocrat from the class of senators, he ended up Rome's head man or proconsul in what is now Turkey. After a stellar career as a diplomat, leading intellectual and Rome's foremost orator, Tacitus retired to the capital, where between AD 114 and 117 he penned his magnificent multi-volume *Annals* of the Roman empire, a detailed account of imperial events in the period AD 14–68. With a first-class education and unfettered access to imperial sources, Tacitus was uniquely placed to write such a history.[7]

Tacitus mentions Jesus only briefly. The crucial lines

are a simple clarification about the origin of the sect of 'Christians'. The only reason he mentions Christians is that this was the group of unfortunates Emperor Nero had blamed for the great fire of Rome, which erupted in the early hours of 19 June AD 64 and spread its fury for nine whole days. By the time the fire was extinguished, three of Rome's fourteen districts were completely destroyed.[8] I want to quote the passage in full, as it gives a vivid insight into what some Christians had to cope with in this period:

> But neither human help, not imperial munificence, nor all the modes of placating Heaven, could stifle scandal or dispel the belief that the fire had taken place by order. Therefore, to scotch the rumour, Nero substituted as culprits, and punished with the utmost refinements of cruelty, a class of men, loathed for their vices, whom the crowd styled Christians.
>
> Christus, the founder of the name, had undergone the death penalty in the reign of Tiberius, by sentence of the procurator Pontius Pilatus, and the pernicious superstition was checked for a moment, only to break out once more, not merely in Judaea, the home of the disease, but in the capital itself, where all things horrible or shameful in the world collect and find a vogue.
>
> First, then, the confessed members of the sect were arrested; next, on their disclosures, vast numbers were convicted, not so much on the count of arson as for hatred of the human race. And derision accompanied their end: they were covered with wild beasts' skins and torn to death by dogs; or they were fastened on crosses, and, when daylight failed were burned to serve as lamps by night.
>
> Nero had offered his Gardens for the spectacle, and gave an exhibition in his Circus [the imperial games arena], mixing with the crowd in the habit of a charioteer, or mounted on his car [i.e., chariot]. Hence, in spite of a guilt which had earned the most exemplary punishment, there arose a sentiment of pity, due to the impression that they were being sacrificed not for the welfare of the state but for the ferocity of a single man.
>
> **Tacitus, *Annals* 15.44**[9]

This nineteenth-century engraving depicts the infamous episode of AD 64 when Nero was said to have played his lyre while Rome burned.

Needless to say, Tacitus was not enamoured of the 'pernicious superstition' of the Christians. But it is precisely his negative attitude towards the movement that makes his remarks so interesting. The main historical importance of the passage is as evidence of Roman antipathy to Christians in the time of Nero (and Tacitus). However, the passing clarification about the execution of the Jew 'Christus'

provides obvious corroboration of other evidence that places Jesus' death during the governorship of Pontius Pilate (AD 26–36).

Pliny (AD 110): Christ as 'god'

Shortly before Tacitus wrote his famous *Annals* another aristocrat wrote a letter to Emperor Trajan seeking advice on the correct procedure for dealing with the followers of Christ. Plinius Caecilius Secundus – Pliny the Younger, for short – was a wealthy Roman senator who held various offices throughout his career, including that of imperial legate (governor) of Bithynia and Pontus in what is now northern Turkey. Around AD 110 Pliny was confronted with the problem of increased public denunciations of Christians in his province. Having never been involved in investigations against this group, he sought the imperial wisdom:

> *The sum total of their guilt or error was no more than the following. They had met regularly before dawn on a determined day, and sung antiphonally [in alternate groups] a hymn to Christ as to a god. They also took an oath not for any crime, but to keep from theft, robbery and adultery, and not to break any promise.*
> **Pliny, *Letters* 10.96**[10]

Until Trajan's answer arrived Pliny did what any self-respecting Roman leader would have done with a reportedly seditious group: he tried and executed the members. He was not completely without human compassion, however, for he also willingly acquitted any accused Christians who performed sacrifices to images of the gods or emperor and who blasphemed Christ. Pliny seems to have thought of Jesus as 'a kind of anti-god to the Roman state gods', write Professors Gerd Theissen and Annette Merz. But he also knows 'that the one worshipped in the cult was a man', since he uses the Latin expression *quasi deo*, 'as a god'. In other words, he 'sees Christ only as a quasi-god, precisely because he was a man'.[11] Pliny provides good evidence that by the beginning of the second century, Christians were widely known to have worshipped the man Christ as divine.

If all we had to work with were these non-Christian references to

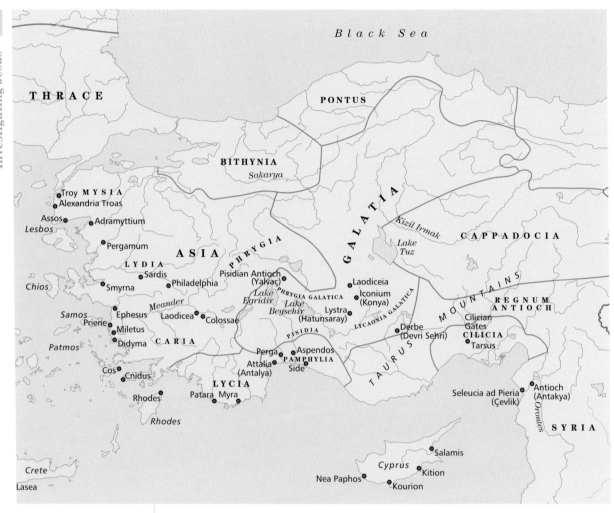

Black Sea

THRACE

PONTUS

BITHYNIA
Sakarya

GALATIA

CAPPADOCIA

Kizil Irmak

Lake Tuz

Troy MYSIA
Alexandria Troas
Assos
Lesbos
Adramyttium

Pergamum

ASIA

PHRYGIA

LYDIA
Sardis
Philadelphia
Pisidian Antioch (Yalvaç)

Chios
Smyrna

PHRYGIA GALATICA

Laodiceia
Iconium (Konya)

REGNUM ANTIOCH

Meander
Lake Egridir
Lake Beysehir

Samos
Ephesus
Laodicea
Colossae
Priene
Miletus
Didyma
CARIA

Lystra (Hatunsaray)

LYCAONIA GALATICA

Cilician Gates

Patmos

PISIDIA

Derbe (Devri Sehri)

CILICIA
Tarsus

MOUNTAINS

TAURUS

Cos
Cnidus
Perga
Aspendos
Attalia (Antalya)
PAMPHYLIA
Side

LYCIA
Rhodes
Patara Myra

Seleucia ad Pieria (Çevlik)
Antioch (Antakya)

Orontes

SYRIA

Rhodes

Crete

Cyprus
Salamis
Kition
Nea Paphos
Kourion

Lasea

Map showing the key towns in Asia Minor (modern-day Turkey) at the time of the reign of Emperor Trajan (AD 98–117).

Jesus from the second century, we would know little more than that he was a Jew living at the time of Pontius Pilate who was (in)famous for his teaching (and sorcery), who was executed by crucifixion and whose followers believed him to be in some way divine. The picture is only slightly enhanced by the first-century references discussed in the next chapter.

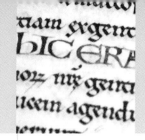

6

CHAPTER

Non-Christian References to Jesus from the First Century

To the three second-century references to Jesus discussed in the previous chapter we can add three more from the first century. Again, they are not all of equal value. Just as Tacitus is considered the most important witness to Jesus from the second century, so Josephus, the first of our authors discussed below, is universally regarded as the most significant non-Christian witness to Jesus from the first century. He is also the most controversial.

Josephus (AD 93): Jesus the teacher, martyr and Christ

Flavius Josephus (AD 37–100) was a Jewish commander in Palestine during the bloody four-and-a-half year war with Rome, which ended in AD 70 with the destruction of Jerusalem and its holy Temple. He led the efforts up north in Galilee where forty years earlier Jesus had lived and worked. When he was captured by the Romans Josephus quickly changed his tune (and sides). He even prophesied that the then Roman commander Vespasian would soon become emperor. The prophecy (or guess) proved correct and the newly appointed emperor granted Josephus not only his freedom but also a generous

What we learn from Josephus

The main importance of Josephus for contemporary scholars is the wealth of information he provides about conditions in Palestine in the Roman period. He also provides confirmation of many of the details of the Gospels concerning figures such as Herod the Great, Pontius Pilate and the high priest Caiaphas. Equally fascinating is his description of the three 'schools' of first-century Judaism:

Jewish philosophy, in fact, takes three forms. The followers of the first school are called Pharisees, of the second Sadducees, of the third Essenes. The Essenes have a reputation for cultivating peculiar sanctity. Of Jewish birth, they show a greater attachment to each other than do the other sects. They shun pleasures as a vice and regard temperance and the control of the passions as a special virtue. Marriage they disdain, but they adopt other men's children, while yet pliable and docile, and regard them as their kin and mould them in accordance with their own principles ...

Of the two first-named schools, the Pharisees, who are considered the most accurate interpreters of the laws, and hold the position of the leading sect, attribute everything to Fate and to God; they hold that to act rightly or otherwise rests, indeed, for the most part with men, but that in each action Fate co-operates. Every soul, they maintain, is imperishable, but the soul of the good alone passes into another body [i.e., resurrection], while the souls of the wicked suffer eternal punishment.

The Sadducees, the second of the orders, do away with Fate altogether, and remove God beyond, not merely the commission, but the very sight, of evil. They maintain that man has the free choice of good or evil, and that it rests with each man's will whether he follows the one or the other. As for the persistence of the soul after death, penalties in the underworld, and rewards, they will have none of them.

The Pharisees are affectionate to each other and cultivate harmonious relations with the community. The Sadducees, on the contrary, are, even among themselves, rather boorish in their behaviour, and in their intercourse with their peers are as rude as to aliens. Such is what I have to say on the Jewish philosophical schools (Josephus, Jewish War 2.119–66).[1]

It is Josephus' references to Jesus, however, that have sparked the most debate.

pension and an apartment in the imperial palace in Rome. It was there between AD 80 and 95 that Josephus wrote his magnificent works *Jewish War* and *Jewish Antiquities*, goldmines of historical information for the period.[1]

The author with the works of Josephus.

I recently had the opportunity to view one of the ten manuscripts of Josephus' works. It is an ornate 900-year-old Latin version of the Greek original and it is lovingly housed in the Special Collections rooms of the Old Library at St John's College, University of Cambridge. I spent a wonderful two hours thumbing through the pages of this large bound volume – a bit bigger than your average city telephone directory and rather more valuable. I could not contain my thrill at handling such an important manuscript of such a famous first-century work.

In section 20 of *Jewish Antiquities* Josephus mentions the execution of several Jewish men in Jerusalem in the year AD 62. After a brief trial before the Sanhedrin (the Jewish court) at the direction of Ananus the high priest, the men were stoned to death as religious 'law-breakers'. Josephus' description of the event would be unremarkable were it not for the passing mention of the *brother* of one of the victims, a certain Jesus:

> *And so he [Ananus the high priest] convened the judges of the Sanhedrin and brought before them a man named James, the brother of Jesus who was called the Christ, and certain others. He accused them of having transgressed the law and delivered them up to be stoned. Those of the inhabitants of the city who were considered the most fair-minded and who were strict in observance of the law were offended at this.*[2]
> **Josephus, *Jewish Antiquities* 20.200**

I have heard people dismiss this text as a forgery inserted into *Jewish Antiquities* by Christians. This is not a view held by

Above: The Latin manuscript of Josephus, *Jewish Antiquities* 20.200.

Right: The Latin manuscript of Josephus, *Jewish Antiquities* 18.63–64.

contemporary scholars, whether Christian, Jewish or agnostic. It is true that a second passage (discussed below) appears to have been 'improved' by Christians, but that should not be confused with the above. There is nothing to suggest a forgery here (unless one begins with the assumption that Jesus did not exist, in which case any mention of him by a non-Christian author is suspicious). The passage fits the context of Josephus' work very well, it shows no real interest in Jesus other than as a convenient way of identifying James, and the expression 'who was called the Christ' does not imply a positive regard for Jesus. Professors Gerd Theissen and Annette Merz express the scholarly consensus well: 'The authenticity of the text may be taken as certain.'[3]

The James referred to here is one of four brothers of Jesus mentioned by name in the New Testament. Three of them (Joseph, Judas and Simon) appear to have become missionaries after Jesus' death but the oldest, James, remained in Jerusalem and led the growing Christian community there.[4] Whereas our New Testament records cut off at about AD 60, when James was still alive, Josephus finishes the story for us. James was martyred in the Holy City.

Most interesting for historians is the fact that Josephus identifies James by referring to his better-known brother Jesus, whom Josephus says 'was called the Christ' (or 'Messiah'). Some scholars, such as Professor Graham Stanton of Cambridge University, translate the original Greek at this point as 'the so-called Christ',

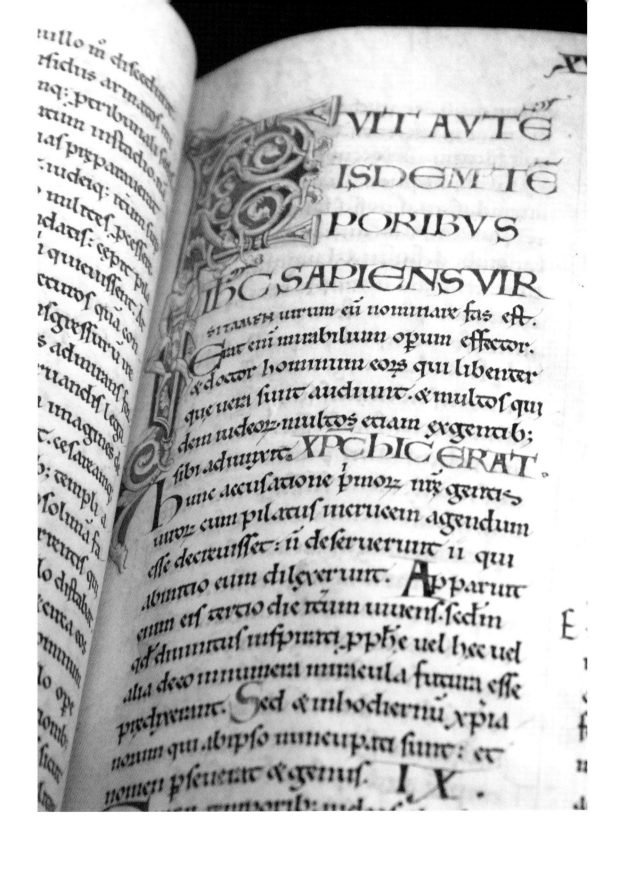

Opposite: *Saint James Dragged to Martyrdom,* by Giovanni Battista Piazetta (1683–1754).

suggesting that Josephus was critical of Christian claims about Jesus.[5] There is no way of knowing this for sure. What we do know is that Josephus was aware of at least four details about Jesus: his name, his popular title and the name and fate of one of his brothers.

In fact, Josephus knew a little more than this. Two sections earlier in *Jewish Antiquities* there is another reference which, on the face of it, offers remarkably positive evidence for Jesus from the pen of a non-Christian:

> *About this time there lived Jesus, a wise man [if indeed one ought to call him a man]. For he was one who wrought surprising feats and was a teacher of such people as accept the truth gladly. He won over many Jews and many of the Greeks. [He was the Messiah.] When Pilate, upon hearing him accused by men of the highest standing amongst us, had condemned him to be crucified, those who had in the first place come to love him did not give up their affection for him. [On the third day he appeared to them restored to life, for the prophets of God had prophesied these and countless other marvellous things about him.] And the tribe of the Christians, so called after him, has still to this day not disappeared.*
> **Josephus, *Jewish Antiquities* 18.63–64[6]**

If you are wondering how on earth a Jewish writer could describe Jesus as the resurrected Christ or Messiah, you are not alone; so do most historians. It really does seem as though somewhere in the copying process the text of Josephus has been altered at this point. A few scholars dispute this, insisting the whole paragraph is authentic.[7] Others go the other way and dismiss the passage as a total forgery.[8] However, the vast majority of experts today adopt a middle position. They believe that Josephus' original words have been 'improved' by some over-zealous Christian scribe who wanted to bring the paragraph into line with official church teachings. The additions may originally have been added as commentary into the margins of a manuscript (which was quite common), only later being incorporated into the body of the text by a copyist who was unsure of the status of the remarks.[9] In any case, I have bracketed the statements believed to be 'improvements'.

What remains in the text – the description of Jesus as a teacher, wonder-worker and martyr – is original to the Jewish historian. Not only are the remaining phrases very much in the style of Josephus, but several of them are unlikely to have come from a Christian. (1) The expression 'a wise man' presents a rather low view of Jesus – this alone probably explains why a later Christian felt the need to add, 'if indeed one ought to call him a man'. (2) 'Surprising feats' translates the Greek *paradoxa erga*, literally 'unusual/baffling deeds', a strange way for a believer to talk of Jesus' healings. (3) Those who condemned Jesus are described in a rather complimentary way as 'men of the highest standing'. (4) The statement that Jesus 'won over many of the Greeks' flatly contradicts what the Gospels (and Paul) say about his ministry to Israel only. (5) It is unlikely that a believer would have said that the Christian tribe 'has still to this day not disappeared,' words which seem to imply an expectation of the movement's demise.[10]

In any case, as already mentioned, no one in antiquity was suggesting that Jesus was a fiction. So, while it is easy to envisage a church scribe altering a statement about Jesus to make it fit with Christian theology, it is difficult to imagine why he would create a 'proof' out of thin air for something no one was yet disputing. Professor Graham Stanton thus states well the current scholarly consensus on this question: 'Once the obvious interpolations are removed this paragraph gives an ambivalent or even mildly hostile assessment of Jesus – one which can be attributed to Josephus with confidence.'[11]

It is probable, in my view, that Josephus gained his information about Jesus and his brother James either in AD 56–62 when he was in Jerusalem or in AD 66–67 when he was stationed in Jesus' home district of Galilee. Either way, what we find in Josephus is another example of the randomness of history. We are simply lucky that a Jewish aristocrat living in the emperor's palace at the end of the first century chose, for reasons unknown, to make passing reference to a relatively minor figure from Palestine decades earlier (Josephus of course was not to know that this man would become a central figure in Western history). 'When we remember that we are hunting for a marginal Jew in a marginal province of the Roman Empire,' writes Professor John Meier, 'it is amazing that a more prominent Jew of the 1st century [Josephus], in no way connected with this marginal Jew's followers, should have

An Arabic version of Josephus

There is evidence that Josephus could have referred to Jesus as the risen Messiah, albeit in a hesitant way. In an Arabic work called *A Universal History*, the tenth-century bishop of Hierapolis named Agapius quotes from the copy of Josephus he had in front of him at the time, a thousand years ago. In this version we do not find the bold affirmation that Jesus *'was* the Messiah' who 'appeared to them restored to life', but merely that 'he was *perhaps* the Messiah' about whom 'they *reported* that he had appeared to them'. The differences are significant, for they cannot easily be described as Christian improvements. What Christian would invent such an indecisive, hesitant account of Jesus' credentials as the *potential* Messiah? To quote the Jewish scholar who brought all this to our attention back in 1971, Professor Shlomo Pines of the Hebrew University of Jerusalem: 'As far as probabilities go, no believing Christian could have produced such a neutral text.'[1] This logic led Shlomo to propose that bishop Agapius may have preserved for us the original form of the Josephus passage at these points,[2] a conclusion endorsed recently by leading New Testament historian Professor James Charlesworth of Princeton Theological Seminary.[3] On this reading Josephus would have referred only in a hesitant or non-committal manner to the claims about Jesus as the risen Christ. This conclusion fits well with the description of Jesus in the other (certain) Josephus passage (*Jewish Antiquities* 20.200): 'Jesus who was *called* the Christ'.[4] Whether or not this is the correct interpretation of the evidence (I change my mind each time I think about it), it must be pointed out that the vast majority of scholars today accept that Josephus did refer to Jesus in *Antiquities* 18.63–64 as a teacher, wonder-worker and victim of crucifixion.

preserved a thumbnail sketch of "Jesus-who-is-called-Messiah".'[12] I suspect that Josephus would be bitterly disappointed to know that out of everything he wrote – his works take up a good half-shelf in my study – just two short paragraphs would occupy so much scholarly attention!

Mara bar Serapion: the wise Jewish king (post-AD 73)

Another unexpected reference to Jesus appears in a letter written from a father to his son sometime shortly after AD 73.[13] Mara bar Serapion (sometimes spelt Sarapion) was an educated Syrian from Samosata in southeast Turkey. We know he was not a Christian (or a Jew) because of his occasional reference to 'our gods' in the plural. From the content of his letter, in which he urges his son to pursue wisdom as the greatest treasure, we can guess that Mara was of Stoic philosophical bent.[14]

There is only one copy of Mara's letter, and it is stored in climate-controlled vaults in the Syriac department of the British Library on Euston Road, London. When I visited the manuscript with a TV crew in 2007 we were chaperoned not only by the curator of the Syriac collection, Dr Vrej Nersessian, but also by an unassuming security guard who watched our every move. Touching the manuscript was restricted, and turning the page forbidden. Every few minutes we were instructed to turn off the camera lights lest the pages suffer heat damage, and only after a designated break were we allowed to resume filming. (It was reassuring to know that ancient documents like this are treated with such seriousness.)

Mara bar Serapion writes from a Roman gaol (there is no mention of where). He warns his son that sometimes even the wise are persecuted by the powerful; he himself is in prison, after all. He offers three historical examples of the principle: Socrates, Pythagoras and an unnamed wise Jewish king:

> *What good did it do the Athenians to kill Socrates, for which deed they were punished with famine and pestilence? What did it avail the Samians[15] to burn Pythagoras, since their country was entirely buried under sand in one moment? Or what did it avail the Jews to kill their wise king, since their kingdom was taken away from them from that time on?*
>
> *God justly avenged these three wise men. The Athenians died of famine, the Samians were flooded by the sea, the Jews were slaughtered and driven from their kingdom, everywhere living in the dispersion.*
>
> *Socrates is not dead, thanks to Plato; nor Pythagoras, because of Hera's statue. Nor is the wise king, because of the new law which he has given.[16]*

Sceptics predictably scramble to find candidates other than Jesus for this 'wise king', but there is very wide agreement among specialists that Mara is indeed referring to Jesus.[17] It just strains belief to imagine there were two figures in first-century Palestine fitting the description: Jew, law-giver, king and martyr (at the hands of his own people). Why Mara fails to name his subject is anyone's guess.

The 'slaughter' and 'dispersion' of the Jews, which Mara implies was fated punishment for killing the wise king, no doubt refers to the events of AD 66–70 when the Romans quashed Palestine and razed Jerusalem to the ground. We know that Christians in this period also believed that the disaster of AD 70 was the result of the Jews' rejection of Jesus, so it is possible Mara got this perspective from Christians themselves. Then again, he could easily have arrived at this conclusion himself by transferring to the Jewish nation what he already believed about the Athenians and the Samians: when you kill a wise

Above: The author with a copy of the letters of Mara bar Serapion.

Left: Ruins of the southern end of the Temple's Western Wall, dating from the era of the fall of Jerusalem.

man, you should expect the worst. Whatever the case, his description of Jesus is quite different from that found in the New Testament. For instance, the repeated phrase 'wise king' is not one of the numerous titles used by Christians in the first century to speak of their Lord. More significantly, Mara says that Jesus lives on not through his resurrection, as Christians taught, but only through his 'new law'. This suggests that Mara's contact with Christians was limited.[18]

Thallos (AD 55): a darkness at the time of Jesus' death

The earliest possible reference to Jesus from the pen of a non-Christian appears in a quotation of the Greek historian Thallos (or Thallus) who, around AD 55, wrote a three-volume history of the eastern Mediterranean in which he apparently referred to the darkness which the Gospels also say covered Judea at the time of Jesus' death. He describes the darkness as a natural eclipse.[19]

Unfortunately, Thallos' opinion on this matter is known to us only through a third-hand report from the ninth century (this doesn't sound promising, I know). Thallos' *Histories* are all lost, but they survived at least to the third century, when a Christian chronicler named Julius Africanus (AD 160–240) wrote his own *World History*, in which he took issue with Thallos' interpretation of the darkness as a natural phenomenon; being a Christian he was sure it was a heavenly sign. To make things more complicated, Julius' work is also lost but sections of it are quoted by the ninth-century Byzantine historian Georgius Syncellus in his *Chronicle*. This one survives. To clarify, what we have here is a ninth-century quotation (Georgius) of a

Christ on the Cross,
by Mihály Munkácsy
(1844–1900).

third-century criticism (Julius) of a first-century historian (Thallos). Julius' criticism of Thallos reads as follows:

> *Thallos calls this darkness an eclipse of the sun. To me this seems illogical.*[20]

When scholarly opinion isn't relevant

I remember well when the British documentary *Jesus: The Evidence* aired on Australian television shortly before the Christmas of 1984. Although raised without any Christian faith, I had started to explore Christianity as a teenager just a year or so earlier. Far from promoting Christ – at Christmas time – the documentary claimed to cast serious doubt over the whole story. The opening voiceover of the programme declared: 'For the last four hundred years New Testament scholarship has steadily eroded confidence in the historical reliability of the Bible and in the image it paints of Jesus as the Son of God.'[1] For a young man with a fledgling faith this was confronting stuff, particularly when one of the well-dressed, accented professors interviewed on the program declared, 'Jesus probably never existed at all.' At the time I was confused.

It was only years later that I discovered (from one of the Ancient History faculty at Macquarie University) that the learned boffin in *Jesus: The Evidence* was none other than London University's professor of German language, George A. Wells, the same man Richard Dawkins continues to cite in support of the possibility that Jesus never lived. The producers of the programme failed to find an expert *within a relevant field* who would deny Jesus' existence and so settled for a scholar from an unrelated discipline, describing him to viewers (just as Dawkins does) simply as 'Professor George Wells of the University of London'. No mention of the fact that Wells is about as qualified to offer expert opinion on the historical Jesus as Richard Dawkins is on the German language or I am on zoology. Professor John P. Meier, one of the leading historians of Jesus today, comes as close as any serious contemporary scholar to 'engaging' with Professor Wells (albeit in a footnote): 'Well's presentation descends to simple affirmation, supported not by argumentation but by citation of generally antiquated authorities … His book … may be allowed to stand as a representative of a whole type of popular Jesus book that I do not bother to consider in detail.'[2] Such is the gap between popular claims and scholarly consensus. It is a gap nowhere more pronounced than in the specific question of the historical value of the New Testament, to which we turn in the next chapter.

Since Jesus was crucified at the Passover full moon, as Julius points out, and solar eclipses cannot naturally occur at the full moon, the event must have been supernatural. It is important to note that Julius does not cite Thallos as proof of the Gospel story. On the contrary, he is defending the Christian interpretation of the darkness against Thallos' naturalistic explanation.

Despite being third-hand, few scholars doubt that Georgius accurately quoted Julius or that Julius was disputing something Thallos actually wrote.[21] The alternative would be to imagine that Georgius invented Julius' criticism of Thallos, or that Julius created an imaginary quarrel with Thallos. This is inherently unlikely in such a passing and disinterested citation. And, as I have said a number of times, there was no plausible motive for ancient Christians to invent 'proofs' of this type (unless we are to imagine they were able to foresee a time when people would question Jesus' very existence and so they created quotations for future benefit).

The question is not whether Thallos' opinion has been correctly recorded but whether his original words included any reference to Jesus and his death. And most experts think they did. For, while it is possible that Thallos referred only to an eclipse (without mentioning Jesus), this would make Julius' retort, 'To me this seems illogical', rather out of place. Had Thallos merely stated that there was an eclipse around the year 30, Julius would have seen it as confirmation of the Gospel story. Instead, he takes issue with the statement. This suggests that, in context, Thallos was denying the supernatural nature of the darkness which coincided with Jesus' death. 'It cannot be proved beyond all doubt that Thallus mentioned the crucifixion of Jesus,' write Professors Gerd Theissen and Annette Merz. 'However, the context in Julius Africanus suggests that contrary to the Christian assertion of a supernatural darkness at the crucifixion of Jesus, Thallus had advanced a "rational" counter-proof by referring to an explicable and datable natural event.'[22]

None of this would prove there really was a darkness (or eclipse) at the time of Jesus' death. Thallos simply provides *possible* evidence that the Christian claim about a heavenly portent coinciding with Jesus' crucifixion was widely enough known by AD 55 to rate a mention and rebuttal from a pagan author.

Why Jesus' life and death cannot reasonably be doubted

As I said at the outset of Chapter 5, it is important not to exaggerate or underestimate the value of these non-Christian sources. The statements are too brief to allow us to construct anything like a 'biography' of Jesus, and the fact that they were composed between thirty and 120 years after Jesus means that they cannot rank alongside the eyewitness testimony we might have hoped for. On the other hand, most of our best sources for things ancient were composed decades after the events they describe – Tacitus' accounts of Caligula and Tiberius are good examples, composed fifty to eighty years after these emperors' deaths. Unless we are going to dismiss most of the reported events of Roman times, we are just going to have to put up with the fact that long time gaps between events and their written record are the norm for ancient history. As I have said already, ancient Mediterranean societies relied more on orality than on literacy. In a period when only 10–15 per cent of the population was literate, the process of oral repetition and memorization, not writing, was the most trusted means of preserving important cultural traditions.[23] This fact alone explains the apparently long time gap of twenty to sixty years between Jesus and the Christian writings about him.

The evidence of the non-Christian sources is sufficient to lead all reputable historians to agree that a Jewish teacher named Jesus really did live and die in the first part of the first century AD. These details are certainly not the domain of 'lovers of impossible debates', as Michel Onfray would have us believe.[24] In fact, there is no academic debate at all. As Professor Christopher Tuckett writes in the famous *Cambridge Companion to Jesus*: 'The fact that Jesus existed, that he was crucified under Pontius Pilate ... seems to be part of the bedrock of historical tradition.' He adds, 'If nothing else, the non-Christian evidence can provide us with certainty on that score.'[25] Reflecting on Tacitus, Josephus and Mara bar Serapion – the three most important non-Christian references to Jesus – Professors Gerd Theissen and Annette Merz conclude their review of the topic with characteristic understatement: 'The mentions of Jesus in ancient historians allay doubt about his historicity.'[26] And, finally, in his new textbook on the subject, New Testament historian

Professor James Charlesworth of Princeton Theological Seminary insists: 'The references to Jesus by a Roman historian [Tacitus] and a Jewish historian [Josephus] disprove the absurd contention that Jesus never lived, a claim made by authors, often not scholars, during the past two hundred years, such as Bruno Bauer, P. L. Couchoud, G. Gurev, R. Augstein, and G. A. Wells.'[27]

7
CHAPTER

The New Testament Records about Jesus

Our search backwards in time to find earlier and earlier sources for Jesus brings us inevitably to what is perhaps the most misunderstood collection of writings from all of ancient history: the New Testament.

Scepticism towards anything 'religious'

The popular scepticism towards the New Testament is based on little more than association. Suspicion towards the church as an institution is carried over into distrust of the church's founding documents. Similarly, disbelief in God is thought to be a reason for dismissing any text which takes God as its starting point. Thus, for Richard Dawkins, 'The only difference between *The Da Vinci Code* and the gospels is that the gospels are ancient fiction while *The Da Vinci Code* is modern fiction.'[1] Unless this is simply a rhetorical flourish, Dawkins here leaves himself vulnerable to the criticism of intellectual dishonesty. I doubt whether he could find a single expert – one teaching and writing in an ancient history department or biblical studies department in a reputable university – who would endorse this sentiment.

The fact is, modern historians do not privilege the New Testament as a divinely inspired text, but neither do they approach it with the

P52, the oldest fragment of the New Testament, dating from AD 125. This text contains parts of John 18.

lazy prejudice that is so common in the popular literature of recent years.[2] As I have already said, most of the great works of the past, from Plato's *Republic* to Newton's *Philosophiae Naturalis Principia Mathematica*, proceed from the assumption that God orders reality. But this does not provide a reason to be suspicious about their earthly content. Scholars are well able to ignore the worldview of an ancient text while assessing it for historical information. Thus, all secular scholars of the historical Jesus disregard the question of whether he was actually the Son of God – a core conviction of the New Testament – and choose only to investigate such things as: What did Jesus teach about himself? What was his dispute with his Jewish contemporaries? What factors led to his execution under Roman law? How did the first Christians come to see him as the risen Messiah? Each of these questions can be explored without recourse to theology or any personal belief in God. They are purely historical questions. Here, the New Testament texts are treated solely as human documents from the first century, no more or less reliable than any other work of similar style and date.

The 'bias' of the Christian records

Closely related to the suspicion about the 'religious' orientation of the New Testament is the charge of bias. These texts were written by people who believed in Jesus; they therefore cannot be trusted to give reliable information about him, so the argument goes. The feeling seems to be, 'Well, they would say that, wouldn't they?'. Not only were the Christians' motives in reporting tainted by their convictions; so too were the original witnesses' memories about Jesus (upon which the whole story was built). I was once challenged on this very point by an intelligent young woman who asked me to list the sources of our knowledge of Jesus. I started with the Roman, Greek and Jewish sources and then turned to the Christian ones now in the New Testament. She stopped me at that point and protested that this literature did not count as historical evidence because it was penned by those who were devoted to Jesus. 'They are unlikely to offer an objective view,' she said. Their memories and their motives were clouded by bias.

'Bias' is present in all writing, ancient or modern, religious or secular. When Tacitus wrote about the emperors, for instance, he was not without an agenda. On the one hand, he was a loyal Roman, passionate about the best traditions of the empire. On the other, he wrote in the wake of the despotic reign of Domitian (AD 81–96) which deeply coloured his accounts of the excesses of the emperors.

Josephus likewise had a point or two to convey. He was a Jewish commander who had basically defected and decided to live in Rome with the emperor. This surely affected his writing. For readers back home in Palestine – who were fewer than he would have liked – he wanted to paint himself as a loyal Jew, but for his majority Greco-Roman readership he hoped to cast Judaism in the best light possible, demonstrating that it was perfectly compatible with good (Roman) order.

Nevertheless, the various biases in Tacitus and Josephus do not make their writings *un*historical. It is not as if historians search and search until they find a text without any angle or agenda. That would rule out virtually every text – with the possible exception of dictionaries and telephone books. The task of the historian is not to discover an agenda-less source but simply to be aware of an author's point of view and take this into account when assessing his or her claims. Bias may colour historical writings but it does not often create them out of nothing. Even the most biased accounts, such as Josephus' description of his defection in the Jewish war, are not to be rejected *in toto*; scholars look for the historical core which such stories invariably contain.

The fact that the first Christians were profoundly affected by Jesus does not mean they were less likely to remember and report the facts about him. The opposite is probably true, according to recent psychological studies of memory. While excessive emotion can impair recollection and even promote false memories, 'in general,' write Professors Daniel Reisberg and Friderike Heuer in *Memory and Emotion*, 'emotion seems to have a positive effect on memory, increasing memory vividness, accuracy,

Can bias be useful?

While an excess of 'bias' creates difficulties for historians, its presence can sometimes be the guarantee of good testimony. Personal attachment to events, far from being a hindrance to historical reporting, often enhances the quality of the evidence. It is a myth (repeated to the point of believability) that a person's emotional involvement in affairs diminishes his or her capacity to recall events correctly. I have a book on my shelf titled *Holocaust Testimonies*,[1] which contains excerpts and analysis of video interviews with survivors of the Nazi atrocities. The full interviews, 1,400 in all, were recorded between 1979 and 1989 and are stored in the Fortunoff Video Archive for Holocaust Testimonies at Yale University in the United States. Although recorded three to four decades after the Second World War, only a fool would dismiss the stunning detail in these interviews – descriptions of persons, conversations, events, sounds and even smells – on the grounds that the witnesses were *too involved* in the affairs to give a true account.

completeness, and longevity'.³ This is the reason modern biographers try to speak to as many close companions of their subject as possible. While objective observers have an important role to play in providing a balanced portrait of an individual, it is those most deeply attached who provide the most significant testimony.

The relevance of all this to New Testament studies has already begun to dawn on scholars. In his 2007 book *Jesus and the Eyewitnesses*, Professor Richard Bauckham reviews recent psychological studies of memory and draws some important conclusions about the New Testament as a record of the first Christians' memories of their beloved master. The original followers of Jesus testified to events (1) in which they were personally involved, (2) which they believed to be greatly significant and which, on anyone's reading, (3) were highly unusual. These are three important predictors of accurate recollection, according to the research Bauckham cites. 'We may conclude', he writes, 'that the memories of eyewitnesses of the history of Jesus score highly by the criteria for likely reliability that have been established by the psychological study of recollective memory.'⁴ The bias of the first witnesses to Jesus cannot be put forward as a reason to dismiss the record of their testimony.

The suspicion of all things religious and the charge of bias are not sufficient or rational grounds for dismissing the New Testament texts as historical sources. The first Christians were well able to report real data about the man at the centre of their worldview. The denial of this is little more than sceptical dogma, the mirror image of the religious dogma sceptics hate so much. The historical approach, as I have said, is neither to privilege the New Testament as a divine text nor to belittle it as less than a human record. Rather, historians examine the sources and claims of the early Christians with the same combination of critical rigour and open-mindedness they accord to the many other writings from the period.

With these caveats in mind, then, we turn now to explore the collection of writings we call the New Testament, keeping in mind that a 'collection' is precisely what it is. For, although these texts appear in a single volume today, they were originally written and disseminated quite separately. When the Gospels of Matthew and Mark were composed, for example, their authors had no idea what was contained in the numerous personal letters the apostle Paul had written to congregations in faraway Thessalonica, Corinth and elsewhere. Likewise, Paul never knew about the Gospels of Matthew and Mark. The story of how these texts came together in the New Testament goes beyond the remit of the present book. For now, it is simply worth remembering that when historians study the New Testament they do not approach it as one source; they read it as a combination of at least six independent witnesses to Jesus.

Paul's epistles (AD 50–65)

If the Gnostic Gospels are our latest sources for Jesus, written 100 to 200 years after their subject, the letters of Paul are the earliest. Paul (formerly Saul) was a one-time persecutor of the early Christians. In the year or so after Jesus' death he made it his personal mission to bring to ruin the followers of the recent false Messiah. However, in the year 31 or 32, while setting out to arrest Christians in Damascus, he encountered the one whose memory he had sought to destroy. He wrote about it himself twenty years later:

> For you have heard of my previous way of life in Judaism, how intensely I persecuted the church of God and tried to destroy it. I was advancing in Judaism beyond many of my own age among my people and was extremely zealous for the traditions of my fathers. But when God, who set me apart from birth and called me by his grace, was pleased to reveal his Son in me so that I might preach him among the Gentiles, my immediate response was not to consult any human being. I did not go up to Jerusalem to see those who were apostles before I was, but I went into Arabia. Later I returned to Damascus.
>
> Then after three years, I went up to Jerusalem to get acquainted with Cephas [Peter] and stayed with him fifteen days. I saw none of the other apostles – only James, the Lord's brother. I assure you before God that what I am writing you is no lie.
>
> **Galatians 1:13–20**

Conversion of Paul depicts the moment when Saul, a Pharisee on the road to Damascus, was converted to God after seeing a great light. Hearing the voice of Jesus, he later changed his name to Paul.

ITALY

Rome
Three Taverns
Forum of Appius
Formia
Fundi
Capua
Puteoli

Tyrrhenian Sea

Rheg

Sicily

Syracuse

Malta

→ Paul's first missionary journey
→ Paul's first missionary return journey
→ Paul's second missionary journey
→ Paul's third missionary journey
→ Paul's third missionary return journey
→ Paul's journey to Rome

0   150 km
0   100 miles

From the moment of this revelation until his death thirty years later Paul devoted himself to promoting what he had once tried to extinguish. He had come to believe that the crucified deceiver was in fact the risen Messiah his own people had been waiting for.

The startling thing about Paul is that, while he was a devout Jew, he felt himself called to preach the news of Jesus beyond his compatriots to the pagans: in his own words, 'so that I might preach him among the Gentiles.'

Paul did not just proclaim Christ like some contemporary travelling evangelist. He also established small groups of converts in each of the towns he visited and appointed leaders to care for them.

Just as there were synagogues scattered throughout the Roman world, so Paul organized a network of churches. And just as in the synagogues, these Christian communities gathered for prayer, Scripture reading, singing of songs and teaching. Paul stayed in touch with these groups through letters, a handful of which have survived. In these epistles he answered their ongoing questions, gave the advice of a father, rebuked his wayward children, praised his readers for their faithfulness in hard times and pleaded them to remain faithful to the message of Jesus they had learned from him.

Over the years Paul has received a lot of bad press. He has been called a bigot, misogynist, conservative and repressive. None of

Paul's missionary journeys are charted below, along with the known churches of the time.

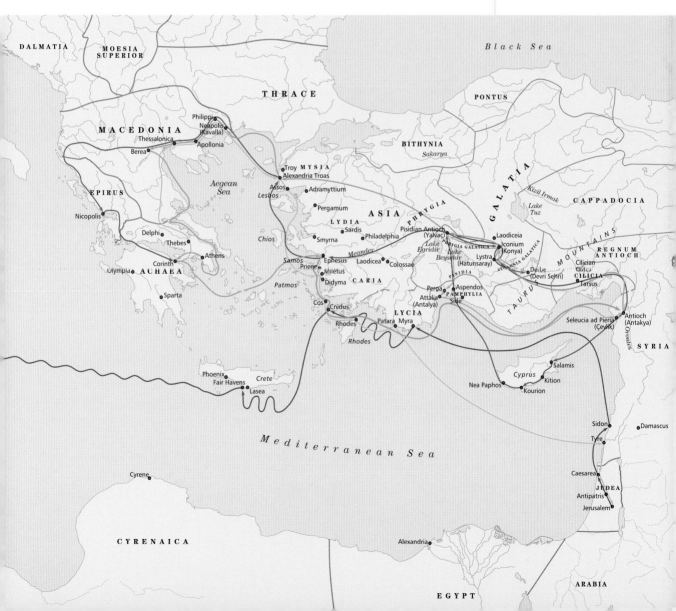

this is warranted. Paul was in fact the great innovator and the true liberal. At the core of his outlook, evident in all of his letters, was the astonishing conviction that God's love extended to the *whole* world, whether Jew or Gentile, slave or free, man or woman, and that this love had shown itself in Jesus' death on behalf of a sinful world. As he says in his letter to the Christians of Rome, 'God demonstrates his own love for us in this: While we were still sinners, Christ died for us' (Romans 5:8). Out of this emphasis on God's lavish love came Paul's equally radical teaching that what God expects of us is not adherence to rules and rituals – even the sacred Jewish traditions – but faith towards God and love for others. He put it starkly in his letter to the Galatians (modern Turkey): 'For in Christ Jesus neither circumcision nor uncircumcision has any value. The only thing that counts is faith expressing itself through love' (Galatians 5:6). Paul preached and wrote of this message until his martyrdom in Rome at the hands of emperor Nero in the early to mid-60s AD.[5]

Romans 4:12 – 5:16 is shown in the Codex Sinaiticus, the oldest complete copy of the New Testament. Dating from the mid-fourth century, it is housed in the British Library, London.

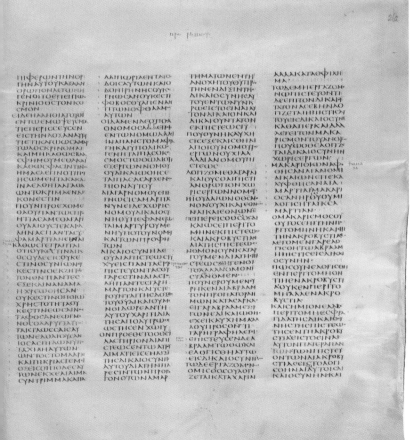

At first glance, Paul's letters are not a very exciting source for the story of Jesus. You will search in vain for anything like a *narrative* description of his birth, teachings or healings, or even his death and resurrection. Buoyed by this observation, Richard Dawkins asserts in *The God Delusion* that the epistles of Paul 'mention almost none of the alleged facts of Jesus' life'.[6] This is a common opinion among popular critics of the New Testament, but the evidence tells a different story.

On closer inspection Paul turns out to be a first-rate witness to the earthly Jesus. The value of his letters lies not in any narration of Jesus' life, such as we have later in the Gospels, but in his numerous *passing* references to Jesus' life while discussing various other topics. He recalls Jesus' teaching on divorce when discussing marriage, he narrates Jesus' sombre Last Supper when criticizing a church for their drunken feasts, and so on. It is perfectly clear in these references that Paul expected his readers to know full well what he was talking about. In other words, he was not *teaching* them about Jesus. He was alluding to material they were already familiar with, as he made fresh observations. His slender evidence, then, turns out to be very significant, for it indicates that what is mentioned in brief in his letters had already been talked about in some detail when Paul first taught his converts face to face years earlier. 'The value of these letters is, first, that they are the earliest Christian sources we can date and localize precisely,' said revered scholar of Paul's writings, Professor Peter Stuhlmacher of the University of Tübingen, in an interview for Australian television in 2008. 'And we find that already there we have the narrative of the Last Supper, we have the message of Jesus crucified, that he was buried, that he was resurrected on the third day after this death, and that he appeared to Peter and others. So the basic data of which the Gospel narratives tell us later, and of course in narrative form, are to be found in Paul's own letters already.'[7]

So, what would we know about Jesus if all we had to go on were Paul's letters? What historical data can we glean from them? The following list is not comprehensive, and more technical works go into much greater detail:[8]

- the name 'Jesus' **(1 Thessalonians 1:1 and just about every other paragraph of his letters)**

- that Jesus was born of a Jewish woman and was therefore a Jew himself **(Galatians 4:4)**

- that his earthly mission focused exclusively on Israel (not the Gentiles) **(Romans 15:8)**

- that he had several brothers **(1 Corinthians 9:5)**, one of whom was named James **(Galatians 1:19)**

- that he appointed a special group of twelve apostles **(1 Corinthians 15:5)**, two of whom, Cephas/Peter and John, acquired special status **(Galatians 2:9)**

- that he was called 'the Christ/Messiah' **(Romans 9:3–5)**

- that he sent out missionaries and granted them the right to material support from fellow believers **(1 Corinthians 9:14)**

- that he forbade divorce **(1 Corinthians 7:10)**, summarized his 'law' as compassion **(Galatians 6:2)** and declared that he would return again in glory **(1 Thessalonians 4:15)**

- that he had a special last meal with his disciples involving bread and wine **(1 Corinthians 11:23–25)**

- that he was betrayed by someone on the night of the Last Supper **(1 Corinthians 11:23)**

The entombment of Jesus is depicted below in *The Entombment*, attributed to sixteenth-century painter Jan Cornelisz Vermeyen.

- that he was executed by crucifixion **(Philippians 2:8)**

- that his body was buried rather than left to the elements (as those of convicted criminals frequently were) **(1 Corinthians 15:4)**

- that he was raised to life **(Romans 1:4)**

- that the risen Jesus appeared to many, including Peter/Cephas, his brother James and Paul himself **(1 Corinthians 15:5–6)**.

We must recall that Paul's letters were not at all intended to inform readers about the life of Jesus (as the Gospels clearly were). Paul simply *assumes* they know the above material already. And *that* is the significant historical point. The narrative of Jesus was so widely known among Christians in the middle of the first century that Paul can allude to all of these details, confident that his readers knew exactly what he was talking about. The passing nature of these references and the occasional nature of Paul's letters mean that, in reality, this list must be the tip of the iceberg of what Paul and his converts really knew about Jesus.[9]

All of this renders quite astonishing an article in the *Australian Rationalist* which repeatedly claimed that the apostle Paul 'knows nothing of the historical Jesus'.[10] Contrast that with the statement of Donald Harman Akenson, Professor of History at Queen's University (Canada), that 'Saul did indeed know his life of the historical Yeshua; that he had a full awareness of the miracle stories, sayings, and of various folk-beliefs about Yeshua'.[11] More impressive is the project of Professor Paula Fredriksen of Boston University. In her *Jesus of Nazareth, King of the Jews* she makes the methodological decision to build her portrait of the historical Jesus from the letters of Paul. Where Paul's statements about Jesus coincide with statements in the Gospels (which were written independently of Paul) and match information about early Judaism from other Jewish sources, such as Josephus or the Dead Sea Scrolls, then we are in a good position to draw historical conclusions about the teacher from Nazareth. After all, writes Fredriksen, 'Beginning our investigation with Paul means beginning with a contemporary of Jesus and his first followers.'[12]

Paul's letters take us to the middle of the first century, twenty years after Jesus. While that is a relatively small time gap by ancient standards, one passage from Paul takes us much closer

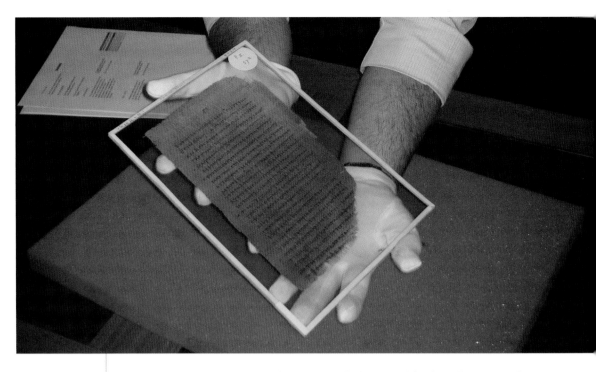

Lines from the earliest manuscript of 1 Corinthians 15, Chester Beatty Library, Dublin.

– to within a few years of the crucifixion. In his first letter to the Corinthians, written about AD 55, Paul stops to remind his readers of the core message he preached to them five years earlier (AD 50). He does this in classic Jewish style by quoting a pithy summary – what we call a creed – which the Corinthians had learned by heart when Paul was with them. Rabbis in this period would often make their disciples learn key mnemonic statements. These were a safeguard to the faith. Paul employed this practice to good effect among his non-Jewish hearers. The key jargon here was *paradidōmi* ('to pass on') and *paralambanō* ('to receive'): one was the duty of the teacher, the other that of the student.[13] But what is fascinating in Paul's quotation from such a creed, below, is that he admits *he* is not the source of the creed. In fact, just as the Corinthians had 'received' it from Paul in AD 50, so Paul had 'received' it from others when he learned of Christ (which we know was in the early to mid-30s AD):

For what I received (paralambanō) I passed on (paradidōmi) to you as of first importance:

that Christ died for our sins according to the Scriptures,
that he was buried,
that he was raised on the third day according to the Scriptures,
and that he appeared to Cephas, and then to the Twelve.
1 Corinthians 15:3–5

Scholars debate precisely when Paul 'received' this creed. Some date it to the very year of his conversion in AD 31/32 (upon arriving in Damascus).[14] Others point to AD 33/34, when he spent fifteen days in Jerusalem in conversation with the apostles Peter and James the brother of Jesus.[15] Whichever date we accept, 'This tradition (1 Corinthians 15:3–5), we can be entirely confident, was formulated as tradition within months of Jesus' death,'[16] writes Professor James Dunn of the University of Durham. Even scholars who openly reject what the creed affirms – that Jesus died 'for our sins' and that he rose again – agree that it must nonetheless be dated to the period almost immediately after the purported events themselves.[17]

I had the privilege of handling the earliest manuscript of this exact passage in the secure and very climate-controlled Chester Beatty Library situated in the gardens of Dublin Castle (Ireland). In my excitement at handling *Papyrus 46*, arguably the most important artefact of early Christianity, I made a fool of myself by asking the curator how much this page in my hand would be worth. He looked quite astonished that this Australian could ask such a thing, and in his most intimidating Queen's English he replied, 'We do not discuss such matters.' Any façade of scholarly decorum on my part was gone.[18]

The significance of this creed quoted by Paul is obvious. It establishes beyond reasonable doubt that the core of the Jesus story was not a developing legend. Already, by the mid-30s AD, Jesus' status as Christ, his death for sins, his burial, his resurrection, his multiple appearances and his appointment of twelve apostles were all sufficiently widely reported to become part of a formal summary of the Christian faith passed on to converts far and wide, whether to Paul in Palestine or to the Corinthians in Greece. This proves – in the historian's sense of the word – that what was later written down in detail in the Gospels was already being proclaimed by missionaries and committed to memory by disciples within months of the alleged events themselves.

Two records of the Last Supper

1 Corinthians 11:23–26

For I received from the Lord what I also passed on to you: The Lord Jesus, on the night he was betrayed, took bread, and when he had given thanks, he broke it and said, 'This is my body, which is for you; do this in remembrance of me.' In the same way, after supper he took the cup, saying, 'This cup is the new covenant in my blood; do this, whenever you drink it, in remembrance of me.'

Luke 22:14–21

When the hour came, Jesus and his apostles reclined at the table. And he said to them, 'I have eagerly desired to eat this Passover with you before I suffer ...'

And he took bread, gave thanks and broke it, and gave it to them, saying, 'This is my body given for you; do this in remembrance of me.'

In the same way, after the supper he took the cup, saying, 'This cup is the new covenant in my blood, which is poured out for you. But the hand of him who is going to betray me is with mine on the table.'

The accuracy of oral tradition in early Christianity can be tested. One of the items Paul mentions in his writings is the Last Supper. In his first letter to the Christians in Corinth, dated to about AD 55, he reminds them of the meal Jesus had with his disciples immediately before being betrayed. The same story is recorded two decades later in the Gospel of Luke. It is important to realize that Luke did not possess a copy of Paul's letter to the Corinthians when he wrote his Gospel a decade after Paul's death. What connected the two renditions of the Last Supper narrative was not a written record of the event but a two-decade-long chain of oral rehearsal and memorization.

There are obvious differences in the two accounts (and no one argues that oral tradition was as accurate as a modern photocopier), but it is strikingly clear in the two accounts that twenty years of rehearsal and memorization have produced no changes affecting the meaning of Jesus' original words. Such was the power of oral tradition. The first Christians sought to preserve the words and deeds of Jesus with the utmost seriousness and through a process which had stood ancient societies in good stead for centuries.

Paul's letters also provide good evidence of the effectiveness of what scholars call 'oral tradition'. In the ancient world, as I mentioned earlier, only 10–15 per cent of the population could read or write. These figures hardly changed until the invention of the printing press in the fifteenth century. Important cultural traditions such as family histories, the teachings of famous philosophers and even national stories were preserved for the

The Supper at Emmaus, 1648, by Rembrandt van Rijn (1606–1669).

masses not in print but through a process of verbal repetition and memorization. This is a major area of study for contemporary scholars and can be explored in depth in numerous volumes, including the important recent work by Professor James Dunn called simply *Jesus Remembered*.[19] The first instinct of the original followers of Jesus was not to write down their accounts of his words and deeds (which would reach only a small minority) but to offer their testimony in public, and repeatedly, urging disciples to rehearse and remember all that they could of the traditions of Jesus. The list of things Paul could expect his readers to know about Jesus (earlier in this chapter) offers a glimpse into the breadth and vitality of this process. It is simply false to imagine that between Jesus and the first writings about him no record of his life was being preserved. It *was* – and through the most trusted means in antiquity, oral tradition.

What we know of oral tradition in antiquity makes clear that the

Leonardo da Vinci's fresco, *The Last Supper* (c. 1495–1497).

first disciples would have had no difficulty in memorizing a great deal of information about Jesus in the decades following his death. Paul's letters provide the evidence that this is indeed what Christians were endeavouring to do in the period before the writing of the Gospels.

With that we turn to the Gospels themselves.

New Testament Gospels (AD 65–100)

Although Paul's letters are the earliest written source for Jesus, the Gospels are universally believed to be the most important. What is a 'Gospel'?

'Gospel' (Greek: *euangelion*) was a media term in the ancient world. It literally means 'good news', but its closest English equivalent would be 'news flash'. Events with significance would be announced to the public as *gospels*. We have examples from the ancient world of gospels concerning military victories, ascensions to the throne, the discovery of the most beautiful girl in the world and even of the bargain-basement price of anchovies at the local market.[20]

The same word was also used by Jews. In the Jewish Scriptures, the Tanakh or Old Testament, 'gospel' referred to the announcement of things God did in history to save his people. So, in the book of Isaiah the prophet speaks of the coming of an anointed herald of good news:

> *The Spirit of the Sovereign Lord is on me,*
> *because the Lord has anointed me*
> *to proclaim good news to the poor.*
> *He has sent me to bind up the brokenhearted,*
> *to proclaim freedom for the captives*
> *and release from darkness for the prisoners,*
> *to proclaim the year of the Lord's favour.*
> **Isaiah 61:1–2**[21]

According to the Gospel of Luke, centuries later Jesus selected this very passage from the Jewish Bible to launch his own mission:

> *He went to Nazareth, where he had been brought up, and on the Sabbath day he went into the synagogue, as was his custom. He stood up to read, and the scroll of the prophet Isaiah was handed to him. Unrolling it, he found the place where it is written:*
>
> *'The Spirit of the Lord is on me,*
> *because he has anointed me*
> *to proclaim good news to the poor ... [etc.]'.*
>
> *Then he rolled up the scroll, gave it back to the attendant and sat down. The eyes of everyone in the synagogue were fastened on him. He began by saying to them, 'Today this scripture is fulfilled in your hearing.'*
> **Luke 4:16–21**

The *bios* genre

Tacitus wrote a *bios* about his father-in-law, Julius Agricola, a famous military commander and one-time governor of Britain.[1] The Greek philosopher Plutarch wrote one about the politician and philosopher Marcus Porcius Cato (the Younger). Suetonius wrote his *Lives of the Caesars*, and Lucian of Samosata penned a *bios* about his revered teacher Demonax, who starved himself to death at the age of 100.[2] The Gospels fit broadly into this genre. Their content was unique – informed by Jewish rather than Greco-Roman ideals – but their form was intelligible to the wider Roman world because of the growing interest at the time in the 'lives' of great men. In her recent review of scholarship on the genre of the Gospels, Professor Loveday Alexander, a classicist, historian and biblical scholar from Sheffield University in the UK, gets the balance just right. She endorses the *bios* consensus about the Gospels with the caveat that, while the external form of the Gospels fits well with the biographical tradition in Greco-Roman culture of the time, it is the special Jewish-Christian oral tradition about Jesus that ultimately shaped the writings we call Gospels.[3]

Jesus understood himself to be the anointed gospel preacher predicted in Isaiah. Indeed, many studies have shown how important Isaiah 61 was for Jesus' understanding of his mission.[22] In any case, the point is simple. The first Christians lived in a world full of 'gospels', but they saw in Jesus' words and deeds the best news flash of all. The opening words of the Gospel of Mark make this clear: 'The beginning of the gospel about Jesus Christ, the Son of God' (Mark 1:1). It made perfect sense, then, to call these books about Jesus 'Gospels'.[23]

That is how the Gospels got their name, but what sort of books are they? American theologian John Shelby Spong would have us believe that the Gospels are not a news flash about real events but *pious fiction* with a spiritual message. 'The concern of the gospel writers was not to record what happened in history,' he assures us, 'but to probe the experience that people had with Jesus.'[24] Bishop Spong seems unaware of the broad consensus of scholarship today that the Gospels are a Jewish-Christian form of the well-known Greco-Roman literary genre of *bios* or biography. This was first argued forcefully by Professor Graham Stanton in 1974,[25] but it was Richard Burridge's 1992 monograph *What are the Gospels?* that changed the scholarly landscape.[26]

The *bios* was not a biography in the modern sense, where authors explore their subjects in intimate detail from cradle to grave. For one thing, the constraints of ancient papyrus meant that these works had to be a lot shorter than their modern counterparts – rarely longer than the Gospels. The ancient *bios* was a rather punchy, straightforward portrait of the deeds and words of great lives. All scholars would agree that ancient biographers had an agenda in retelling their stories: often they wanted to convey a moral or philosophical point. But there is no question but that they were also setting out to tell *real* episodes from the subject's life.

The Gospels too had a message for the world, an agenda; but it was not simply to probe what it means to 'experience the Christ-Spirit', as Spong thinks. They had a gospel to announce – a news flash – which had everything to do with the actual words and deeds of a particular man. 'The importance of that', says Professor Richard Bauckham, reflecting on this point, 'is that they (the original readers of a Gospel) would expect this to be a record of what happened. They would not have expected it to be mere legend or an entertaining bit of fiction or other kinds of literature you could be reading. The Gospels look like the biography.'[27]

The unbiased historian gladly places more confidence in these Jewish-Christian biographies than is often realized. In his discussion of Matthew, Mark and Luke, Jewish scholar David Flusser, Professor of History of Religion at the Hebrew University (Jerusalem), remarked:

> *The early Christian accounts about Jesus are* not *as* untrustworthy *as people today often think. The first three gospels not only present a reasonably faithful picture of Jesus as a Jew of his own time, but consistently maintain his style of speaking about himself in the third person.*[28]

8

CHAPTER

Sources in the Gospels

In constructing their works, ancient biographers often used earlier sources. Professor Richard Burridge of King's College London writes:

> *Many possible sources were used by ancient writers in composing their works, as we know from their own descriptions of their work, as well as from direct source analysis and criticism. Written sources include historical documents, archives, letters, treatises, histories, biographies, inscriptions, collections of sayings ... Oral traditions were highly respected within a less literate society and could include family memories and precedents, stories, eyewitness accounts, personal memories, the tradition of a school or group, anecdotes and so on.*[1]

The Gospels also used sources in writing their particular kind of *bios*. These included earlier accounts of Jesus' life, lists of sayings, collections of miracle stories and parables, and oral tradition, including eyewitness testimony. In a passage quoted earlier, Luke opens his Gospel with a clear statement of his investigation of prior sources:

> *Many have undertaken to draw up an account of the things that have been fulfilled among us, just as they were handed down to us by those who from the first were eyewitnesses and servants*

*of the word. With this in mind, since I myself have carefully
investigated everything from the beginning, I too decided to
write an orderly account for you, most excellent Theophilus,
so that you may know the certainty of the things you have
been taught.*
Luke 1:1–4

Who were the 'many' who, according to Luke, had already put pen
to papyrus by the time he produced his Gospel in the mid-70s AD?
One person, in the opinion of virtually all scholars, was Mark, who, a
decade earlier, had authored the Gospel of Mark.

The Gospel according to Mark (AD 65–75)

A careful analysis of the Gospels of Luke and Matthew suggests that
both writers used the Gospel of Mark as a basis for their own work on
Jesus. Large portions of Mark are quoted virtually unchanged in the
other two Gospels: 80 per cent of Mark appears in Matthew and about
60 per cent in Luke.

Why did Luke and Matthew defer so much to Mark's Gospel? One
reason is found in a comment from Papias, bishop of Heirapolis
(AD 60–130). He makes clear that the Gospel of Mark was penned by
an intimate colleague of the apostle Peter, the chief eyewitness of
Jesus' life:

*Mark became Peter's interpreter and wrote accurately all that
he remembered, not, indeed, in order, of the things said or done
by the Lord. For he had not heard the Lord, nor had he followed
him, but later on, as I said, followed Peter, who used to give
teaching as necessity demanded but not making, as it were, an
arrangement of the Lord's oracles, so that Mark did nothing
wrong in thus writing down single points as he remembered
them. For to one thing he gave attention, to leave out nothing of
what he had heard and to make no false statements in them.*[2]

A generation ago scholars were dismissive of what Papias said about
the Gospel of Mark. They thought he was just trying to make the

Gospel sound more authoritative by inventing a 'Mark' who had a solid connection to the apostle Peter. This view is less credible and less widely believed today. Professor Martin Hengel had shown it to be based on little more than knee-jerk scepticism.[3] Papias' report is very early, taking us to the last decade of the first century. Moreover, it lacks entirely the apologetic character we would expect if this were simply an attempt to elevate the importance of Mark's Gospel by associating it with a man who knew Peter. Papias is actually quite reserved about Mark, even suggesting there is something not quite right in his 'arrangement' of the story.[4] He also makes clear that Mark was not an eyewitness. If this really were an invention designed to enhance the authority of Mark's Gospel, why not just make him another eyewitness?

An eyewitness source

In his groundbreaking *Jesus and the Eyewitnesses* (2006), Richard Bauckham has shown that the Gospel of Mark itself contains indicators that it is based on the eyewitness account of Peter. By making Peter the *first* disciple named in his work (Mark 1:16) and the *last* (Mark 16:7), Mark has created what is called an '*inclusio*', literary bookends, designed to specify who his eyewitness source was, a practice used by other ancient authors. 'The Gospel of Mark itself,' writes Bauckham, 'by means of the literary device of *inclusio* of eyewitness testimony, indicates that Peter was the principal eyewitness source of this Gospel.'[1] This, says Bauckham, provides a 'most important reason for reconsidering Papias' evidence'.[2]

We can now see why Luke and Matthew would be so keen to use Mark as a basis for their own work. They were not simply plagiarizing to make the job easier. They were grounding their story in a prior authority. What better basis for a narrative outline of Jesus' life than the reported testimony – the oral tradition – of Jesus' leading apostle, Peter?[5] The example in Table 1 (opposite) provides a taste of Mark's Gospel and shows just how closely (and yet imprecisely) Matthew and Luke follow that source in their own works. The Gospel of Mark is not the only source behind the Gospels of Matthew and Luke. Scholars detect three further sources, known by the letters Q, L and M.[6]

The Gospel source known as Q (AD 40–70)

'Q' is short for the German word Quelle or source. It refers to material in the Gospels of Matthew and Luke which seems to have

A parallel account in Mark, Matthew and Luke

Mark 1:29–34

As soon as they left the synagogue, they went with James and John to the home of Simon and Andrew. Simon's mother-in-law was in bed with a fever, and they immediately told Jesus about her. So he went to her, took her hand and helped her up. The fever left her and she began to wait on them. That evening after sunset the people brought to Jesus all the sick and demon-possessed. The whole town gathered at the door, and Jesus healed many who had various diseases.

Matthew 8:14–16

When Jesus came into Peter's house, he saw Peter's mother-in-law lying in bed with a fever. He touched her hand and the fever left her, and she got up and began to wait on him.

When evening came, many who were demon-possessed were brought to him, and he drove out the spirits with a word and healed all the sick.

Luke 4:38–40

Jesus left the synagogue and went to the home of Simon. Now Simon's mother-in-law was suffering from a high fever, and they asked Jesus to help her. So he bent over her and rebuked the fever, and it left her. She got up at once and began to wait on them. At sunset, the people brought to Jesus all who had various kinds of sickness, and laying his hands on each one, he healed them.

Left: Table 1.

Below: The ruins at Capernaum. The town, near Lake Galilee, was the base for Jesus' ministry, and the site of the events mentioned in Table 1.

come from another pre-existing document. This extra material has no parallel in Mark and yet appears almost word for word in the other two Gospels. Scholars therefore rightly ask: where did this material come from? One answer, suggested by a significant number of scholars, is to say that Luke copied Matthew (or that Matthew copied Luke). However, most experts judge this to be unlikely, because in other important respects Matthew and Luke are very different from each other and appear to have been written independently. The most plausible solution is to suppose that Matthew and Luke shared another source in addition to the Gospel of Mark. That source is known as Q.

An illustration may help explain the logic of Q. Imagine two of my students handed in essays which were very different from each other in style, theme and conclusion and yet which contained about ten paragraphs scattered throughout the paper with near-identical wording. What would I conclude? The great differences between the pieces would suggest that the one was not simply copied from the other, but the identical passages would strongly indicate some common source. I would have to conclude that both students, independently of each other, had stumbled across the same journal article, textbook or web page and then worked it into their respective essays in different ways. Even if I were unable to track down the source, my hypothesis would still be the easiest explanation. Likewise, most scholars believe Q really did once exist, even though they hold out little hope of it ever being discovered. 'It's absolutely certain', says Professor Christopher Tuckett, one of the leading Q experts, 'that there were other documents around the place in early Christianity that have now got lost. Some of them have got lost and we know about them (for example, Q); others have got lost and we don't know about them.'[7]

The quotations from Matthew and Luke in Table 2 (opposite) are generally believed to derive from Q, a document that seems to have focused on the teachings of Jesus rather than on his deeds. You will notice small differences of wording and arrangement in the two versions, but the use of a common source is obvious.

Matthew 5:38–48	Luke 6:27–36
'You have heard that it was said, "Eye for eye, and tooth for tooth." But I tell you, do not resist an evil person. If anyone slaps you on the right cheek, turn to them the other cheek also. And if anyone wants to sue you and take your shirt, hand over your coat as well. If anyone forces you to go one mile, go with them two miles. Give to the one who asks you, and do not turn away from the one who wants to borrow from you. 'You have heard that it was said, "Love your neighbour and hate your enemy." But I tell you, love your enemies and pray for those who persecute you, that you may be children of your Father in heaven. He causes his sun to rise on the evil and the good, and sends rain on the righteous and the unrighteous. If you love those who love you, what reward will you get? Are not even the tax collectors doing that? And if you greet only your own people, what are you doing more than others? Do not even pagans do that? Be perfect, therefore, as your heavenly Father is perfect.'	But to you who are listening I say: Love your enemies, do good to those who hate you, bless those who curse you, pray for those who mistreat you. If someone slaps you on one cheek, turn the other also. If someone takes your coat, do not withhold your shirt. Give to everyone who asks you, and if anyone takes what belongs to you, do not demand it back. Do to others as you would have them do to you. 'If you love those who love you, what credit is that to you? Even sinners love those who love them. And if you do good to those who are good to you, what credit is that to you? Even sinners do that. And if you lend to those from whom you expect repayment, what credit is that to you? Even sinners lend to sinners, expecting to be repaid in full. But love your enemies, do good to them, and lend to them without expecting to get anything back. Then your reward will be great, and you will be children of the Most High, because he is kind to the ungrateful and wicked. Be merciful, just as your Father is merciful.'

Before we go any further I would like to make two very important points about the sources in the Gospels. First, we should not think that the Gospel writers' 'copying' of prior documents was in any way dishonest or unethical. The modern notion of plagiarizing should not be imposed on this discussion, for in the ancient world it was fully expected that histories and biographies would draw on earlier authorities without following today's convention of citing sources. Even without Luke's opening declaration that 'many have undertaken to draw up an account' of Jesus' life, we would expect the Gospel writers to weave earlier sources into their works.

Second, in the case of Matthew and Luke we are able to observe how faithfully they reproduce their sources. If you compare their use of Q in the above quotation, or their use of Mark in the quotation

Above: Table 2.

given in Table 1, it is quite obvious that Matthew and Luke are *traditionalists*, not innovators. Their habit is to reproduce pre-existing material about Jesus accurately. Differences do exist, as the quotations in Tables 1 and 2 also make clear; indeed, there is an entire discipline in New Testament studies called 'redaction criticism', which analyses Matthew's and Luke's editing (or redaction) of Mark and Q. But the variations are small compared to the similarities. Luke and Matthew would never have imagined how closely modern scholars would cross-check their work, line by line. They pass the test with flying colours.

This last observation allows scholars to feel confident about Matthew's and Luke's use of other sources in the Gospels which we cannot now cross-check. Such is the case with L and M.

A source in the Gospel of Luke, known as L (AD 40–70)

Most scholars believe the Gospel of Luke was composed sometime between AD 75 and 85 – though some date it before the year 70.[8] Luke in fact wrote two volumes now in the New Testament, one dealing with the life of Jesus, and the other tracing the work of the first Christians after Jesus up to about AD 62. This is known as the book of Acts, and it is in this work that we learn that Luke himself was an intermittent missionary companion of the apostle Paul as early as AD 49. This places him among key Christian figures of the first generation. In his first-hand account of the events of AD 49 he writes, 'After Paul had seen the vision, we got ready at once to leave for Macedonia, concluding that God had called us to preach the gospel to them' (Acts 16:10). This passage is the first of the so called 'we sections' in the book of Acts. Here the author suddenly moves from third-person narration to first-person reporting. The change is dramatic. Some have interpreted this simply as Luke's rather wooden use of an earlier eyewitness source written by someone else. This is highly improbable. Luke's Gospel provides ample evidence that he was well able to weave his sources into a seamless narrative. The far more satisfactory explanation, accepted by most today, is that Luke was an active participant in the events recounted in Acts 16:10–17; 20:5–15; 21:1–18 and 27:1 – 28:16, that is, between AD 49

and 51, 54 and 57, and 59 and 62.

'The remarks in the first person plural refer to the author himself. They do not go back to an earlier independent source, nor are they a mere literary convention, giving the impression that the author was an eyewitness.' So writes Martin Hengel in his classic treatment of historical issues in the book of Acts. He continues: 'From the beginning, this is the only way in which readers – and first of all Theophilus, to whom the two-volume work was dedicated and who must have known the author personally – could have understood the "we" passages. "We" therefore appears in travel accounts because Luke simply wanted to indicate that he was there.'[9] Luke, in other words, was well placed to write a history of Jesus (and of the early church), given his close association with the first generation of Christian leaders.

The oldest fragments of Acts 20:30–37 and 2:46 – 3:2, housed at the Museum of Ancient Cultures, Macquarie University, Sydney.

We have already seen that Luke's Gospel depends in large part on the prior sources of Mark and Q, which probably date from a decade (or more in the case of Q) earlier. But that is not the end of the matter. There is a fair amount of material in Luke which does not come from Mark or Q, and which is in fact unique to his Gospel. Where did it come from? A decided sceptic might answer that Luke simply invented stories about Jesus. However, few scholars today think this is likely to any significant degree. For one thing, Luke's rather conservative use of Mark and Q suggests that creating material out of nothing was not his style. 'The general fidelity of Luke to his sources', writes Professor I. Howard Marshall of the University of Aberdeen, a leading expert on Luke's writings, 'makes one skeptical of suggestions that he created material in the Gospel on any large scale.'[10]

Just as importantly, much of this additional material in Luke (i.e., material not derived from Mark or Q) betrays a particular linguistic and thematic style, and this style can be distinguished from Luke's own editorial hand when he, for example, introduces his Gospel, writes transitions between episodes or offers commentary on something Jesus did.[11] This leads the majority of scholars to suppose that, in addition to Mark and Q, Luke used another pre-existing source now lost to us. It is known as 'Luke's special source', or simply L.

Feast in the House of Simon, by Sandro Botticelli (c. 1445–1510).

Roughly one third of the Gospel of Luke is believed to derive from L. It contains some wonderful parables and stories of Jesus. Among my favourite are the following:

As Jesus and his disciples were on their way, he came to a village where a woman named Martha opened her home to him. She had a sister called Mary, who sat at the Lord's feet listening to what he said. But Martha was distracted by all the preparations that had to be made. She came to him and asked, 'Lord, don't you care that my sister has left me to do the work by myself? Tell her to help me!'

'Martha, Martha,' the Lord answered, 'you are worried and upset about many things, but few things are needed – or indeed only one. Mary has chosen what is better, and it will not be taken away from her.'

Luke 10:38–42

[Luke begins with his own editorial transition.] Now on his way to Jerusalem, Jesus travelled along the border between Samaria and Galilee. [Then begins his story from L.] As he was going into a village, ten men who had leprosy met him. They stood at a distance and called out in a loud voice, 'Jesus, Master, have pity on us!'

When he saw them, he said, 'Go, show yourselves to the priests.' And as they went, they were cleansed.

One of them, when he saw he was healed, came back, praising God in a loud voice. He threw himself at Jesus' feet and thanked him – and he was a Samaritan.

Jesus asked, 'Were not all ten cleansed? Where are the other nine? Was no one found to return and give praise to God except this foreigner?' Then he said to him, 'Rise and go; your faith has made you well.'

Luke 17:11–19

[Luke begins with his own editorial introduction.] Now the tax collectors and sinners were all gathering around to hear him [Jesus]. But the Pharisees and the teachers of the law muttered, 'This man welcomes sinners and eats with them.'

Then Jesus told them this parable [then begin two parables from L]: 'Suppose one of you has a hundred sheep and loses one of them. Doesn't he leave the ninety-nine in the open country and go after the lost sheep until he finds it? And when he finds it, he joyfully puts it on his shoulders and goes home. Then he calls his friends and neighbours together and says, "Rejoice with me; I have found my lost sheep." I tell you that in the same way there will be more rejoicing in heaven over one sinner who repents than over ninety-nine righteous persons who do not need to repent.

'Or suppose a woman has ten silver coins and loses one. Doesn't she light a lamp, sweep the house and search carefully until she finds it? And when she finds it, she calls her friends and neighbours together and says, "Rejoice with me; I have found my lost coin." In the same way, I tell you, there is rejoicing in the presence of the angels of God over one sinner who repents.'

Luke 15:1–10

These and other passages from L tend to highlight 'Jesus as an authoritative teacher of God's radical, free grace,' says Professor Robert E. Van Voorst in his volume *Jesus Outside the New Testament*, published in 2000. Other Gospel sources also refer to Jesus' openness to sinners and outcasts, but this theme receives particular emphasis here in Luke's special source.

A source in the Gospel of Matthew, known as M (AD 40–80)

Most date the Gospel of Matthew to around AD 80–95,[12] though, again, a few prominent scholars believe it was written before AD 70 and contains much that derives from the teaching of the apostle Matthew himself.[13] All our manuscripts of this work contain the words KATA MATTHAION ('according to Matthew') in the title, indicating that from the earliest days Christians associated the Gospel with the disciple of Jesus named Matthew.

Saint Matthew and the Angel (c.1602), by Michelangelo Merisi da Caravaggio.

Like Luke, Matthew has a great deal of material which does not come from his two primary sources, Mark and Q, and which is unique to his Gospel. This material is usually known as Matthew's special source or M. Unlike Luke's special source, however, M is not so easily thought of as a *collection* of material. Rather, as leading Matthean scholars W. D. Davies and Dale C. Allison note in their magisterial three-volume commentary on the Gospel, 'M' is best used as 'a convenient symbol for a plurality of sources, for those sources behind Matthew – oral and/or written – which cannot be identified with Mark, Q, or Matthean redaction'.[14] Key passages in the Gospel of Matthew usually thought to derive from M include the following:

'You have heard that it was said to the people long ago, "You shall not murder, and anyone who murders will be subject to judgment." But I tell you that anyone who is angry with a brother or sister will be subject to judgment. Again, anyone who says to a brother or sister, "Raca," is answerable to the Sanhedrin. And anyone who says, "You fool!" will be in danger of the fire of hell.

'Therefore, if you are offering your gift at the altar and there remember that your brother or sister has something against you, leave your gift there in front of the altar. First go and be reconciled to that person; then come and offer your gift.'
Matthew 5:21–24

'At that time the kingdom of heaven will be like ten virgins who took their lamps and went out to meet the bridegroom. Five of them were foolish and five were wise. The foolish ones took their lamps but did not take any oil with them. The wise, however, took oil in jars along with their lamps. The bridegroom was a long time in coming, and they all became drowsy and fell asleep.

'At midnight the cry rang out: "Here's the bridegroom! Come out to meet him!"

'Then all the virgins woke up and trimmed their lamps. The foolish ones said to the wise, "Give us some of your oil; our lamps are going out."

'"No," they replied, "there may not be enough for both us and you. Instead, go to those who sell oil and buy some for yourselves."

'But while they were on their way to buy the oil, the bridegroom arrived. The virgins who were ready went in with him to the wedding banquet. And the door was shut.

'Later the others also came. "Sir! Sir!" they said. "Open the door for us!"

'But he replied, "Truly I tell you, I don't know you."

'Therefore keep watch, because you do not know the day or the hour.'
Matthew 25:1–13

A source in the Gospel of John, known as SQ (AD 50–70)

The last of the Gospels to be composed, in the opinion of most experts, was John. It was probably written between AD 90 and 100, that is, sixty to seventy years after Jesus' death. If this seems like a long time gap, it should be remembered that it is still quite a bit shorter than the gap between Jesus and the earliest of the Gnostic Gospels (Thomas, AD 125–40). It is also roughly equivalent to the time gap between Emperor Tiberius, who died in AD 37, and our most important imperial witness to his life, Tacitus (AD 115).

In any case, many scholars (though by no means all) detect an earlier source within the Gospel of John. They call it the Signs Source or SQ for short (SQ stands for *Semeia Quelle*: the Greek word for 'signs' with the German word for 'source'). SQ appears to have been a collection of seven miracle stories or *signs* highlighting Jesus' status as Messiah.[15] Two of the signs are numbered. After the famous water-into-wine miracle, we read: 'What Jesus did here in Cana of Galilee was the first of the signs through which he revealed his glory' (John 2:11). After the healing of a man's son two chapters later the text adds, 'This was the second sign Jesus performed after coming from Judea to Galilee' (John 4:54). Five more miracle stories are then narrated (but without this numbering system). Then, towards the end of John's Gospel, we read what many scholars think was the conclusion to the Signs Source: 'Jesus performed many other signs in the presence of his disciples, which are not recorded in this book. But these are written that you may believe that Jesus is the Messiah, the Son of God, and that by believing you may have life in his name' (John 20:30–31). (The conclusion of the Gospel proper comes a chapter later.) In other words, a short book listing seven signs of Jesus' messianic status appears to have been incorporated into the much longer Gospel of John. The following passages are generally believed to come from SQ:

> *On the third day a wedding took place at Cana in Galilee. Jesus' mother was there, and Jesus and his disciples had also been invited to the wedding. When the wine was gone, Jesus' mother said to him, 'They have no more wine.'*

'Woman, why do you involve me?' Jesus replied. 'My hour has not yet come.'

His mother said to the servants, 'Do whatever he tells you.'

Nearby stood six stone water jars, the kind used by the Jews for ceremonial washing, each holding from twenty to thirty gallons.

Jesus said to the servants, 'Fill the jars with water'; so they filled them to the brim.

Then he told them, 'Now draw some out and take it to the master of the banquet.'

They did so, and the master of the banquet tasted the water that had been turned into wine. He did not realize where it had come from, though the servants who had drawn the water knew. Then he called the bridegroom aside and said, 'Everyone brings out the choice wine first and then the cheaper wine after the guests have

The Marriage at Cana (1819), by Julius Schnorr von Carolsfeld.

had too much to drink; but you have saved the best till now.'

What Jesus did here in Cana of Galilee was the first of the signs through which he revealed his glory, and his disciples put their faith in him.

John 2:1–11

Now there is in Jerusalem near the Sheep Gate a pool, which in Aramaic is called Bethesda and which is surrounded by five covered colonnades. Here a great number of disabled people used to lie – the blind, the lame, the paralysed. One who was there had been an invalid for thirty-eight years. When Jesus saw him lying there and learned that he had been in this condition for a long time, he asked him, 'Do you want to get well?'

'Sir,' the invalid replied, 'I have no one to help me into the pool when the water is stirred. While I am trying to get in, someone else goes down ahead of me.'

Then Jesus said to him, 'Get up! Pick up your mat and walk.' At once the man was cured; he picked up his mat and walked.

John 5:2–9

Summary of sources

The discussion of sources in the last four chapters may seem overly technical and confusing. This table lays out the Christian and non-Christian sources in reverse chronological order, from latest to earliest.

AD 150–200	Talmud: *baraitha Sanhedrin*	A second-century Jewish reference to Jesus as a rightly executed deceiver and sorcerer (see Chapter 5 above).
AD 125–300	Gnostic Gospels: Philip, Judas, Thomas, etc.	While most of the Gnostic Gospels provide little or no information about Jesus himself, the Gospel of Thomas probably contains half a dozen authentic sayings of Jesus (see Chapter 4 above).
AD 115	Tacitus	An important Roman reference to Jesus' death and the 'deadly superstition' he launched (see Chapter 5).
AD 110	Pliny the Younger	A passing reference from a Roman official to the Christian worship of Christ 'as a god' (see Chapter 5 above).

AD 93	Josephus	Two important references to Jesus from the hand of the great Jewish historian. Jesus appears as a teacher, wonder-worker and martyr who was called by some 'Christ' (see Chapter 6).
AD 80–100	Gospel of John	The latest of the New Testament Gospels offering a complete biography of Jesus and employing at least one earlier source, SQ (see above in this chapter).
AD 80–95	Gospel of Matthew	A complete New Testament biography of Jesus incorporating at least three earlier sources, Mark, Q and M (see in this chapter).
AD 75–85	Gospel of Luke	A complete New Testament biography of Jesus incorporating at least three earlier sources, Mark, Q, L (see in this chapter).
AD 73–90	Mara bar Serapion	A stoic writer's probable reference to Jesus as the wise Jewish king and martyr (see Chapter 6).
AD 65–75	Gospel of Mark	A complete New Testament biography of Jesus probably dependent on the testimony of the apostle Peter (see in this chapter).
AD 55	Thallos	Probable Greek reference to a darkness coinciding with the death of Jesus (see Chapter 6).
AD 50–70	SQ	The Signs Source in John's Gospel narrating seven miracles which highlight Jesus' status as Messiah (see in this chapter).
AD 50–65	Letters of Paul	An early New Testament witness to numerous details of Jesus' life. One passage, 1 Corinthians 15:3–5, quotes a creed dated to the middle of the 30s AD (see Chapter 7).
AD 40–80	M	The special source in Matthew's Gospel containing various teachings and parables (see in this chapter).
AD 40–70	Q	A source behind Matthew and Luke containing mainly teachings of Jesus (see in this chapter).
AD 40–70	L	The special source in Luke's Gospel containing a number of parables, stories and teachings of Jesus (see in this chapter).
AD 31–35	1 Corinthians 15:3–5	An oral creed (learned and quoted by Paul) referring to Jesus' death, burial, resurrection, appearances and status as Messiah (see Chapter 7).

9

CHAPTER

Testing the Gospel Story

In Chapter 7 we looked at the question of bias. We saw there that historians are well used to handling texts written from a strong perspective, whether those of Josephus, Tacitus or the New Testament. Part of the reason historians are not overly concerned with the obvious biases in their sources is that they have developed a number of tests for assessing reliability. What follows is a brief account of the criteria of historicity modern scholars employ when reading the New Testament.

The criterion of dissimilarity

I briefly mentioned the criterion of dissimilarity in Chapter 2, when we discussed the twentieth-century quest for Jesus. This test insists that parts of the Jesus story which are different from both ancient Judaism and the early Christian church can be accepted as historical. The logic here is twofold: (1) if a story or teaching of Jesus was reminiscent of later church teachings or practice, it may well have been a simple justification of church tradition written back into the story of Jesus; (b) if a teaching or story of Jesus resonated with the Judaism of the time, it may well have been an invention designed to make Jesus fit with Jewish culture.

The criterion has been heavily criticized in the last thirty years because it assumes (1) that Jesus was not very Jewish and (2) that he had little or no impact on the beliefs and practices of his followers.

Both are patently absurd, and it is bizarre that some scholars still take it so seriously. Most do not.[1]

It is now widely recognized that the criterion of dissimilarity has only *positive* force. That is, it can affirm the plausibility of parts of the Jesus story but it cannot disprove them. How so? When a teaching of Jesus recorded in the Gospels is different from both ancient Judaism and the early church, we can be fairly confident it is historical, since it is unlikely the Gospel writers would have invented an idea foreign to their cultural and religious context. But it does not follow from this that a teaching which *does* resonate with Judaism and/or the early church is unhistorical. Jesus did not live in a vacuum. He had a heritage from his Jewish culture and he had a huge impact on his followers. The famous Lord's Prayer provides a good example of why the criterion of dissimilarity should not be used negatively:

> *Our Father in heaven,*
> *hallowed be your name,*
> *your kingdom come,*
> *your will be done*
> *on earth as it is in heaven.*
> *Give us today our daily bread.*
> *And forgive us our debts,*
> *as we also have forgiven our debtors.*
> *And lead us not into temptation,*
> *but deliver us from the evil one.*
> **Matthew 6:9–13**

Many of the phrases in this prayer can be found in Jewish writings from the period. We also know that the early Christians recited this prayer frequently. Does this mean that it did not come from Jesus, that it was invented by Christians? Definitely not. If the Jewish teacher Jesus did teach his disciples a prayer – as other rabbis did – it is highly probable (1) that he would use Jewish phraseology and (2) that his disciples would continue to use it. The negative application of the criterion of dissimilarity is thus shown to be misguided.

Jesus' prohibition of oaths provides a good example of the *positive* application of the criterion of dissimilarity. In the Gospel of Matthew the following saying of Jesus' is recorded:

'Again, you have heard that it was said to the people long ago, "Do not break your oath, but fulfil to the Lord the vows you have made." But I tell you, do not swear an oath at all: either by heaven, for it is God's throne; or by the earth, for it is his footstool; or by Jerusalem, for it is the city of the Great King. And do not swear by your head, for you cannot make even one hair white or black. All you need to say is simply "Yes," or "No"; anything beyond this comes from the evil one.'
Matthew 5:33–37

This teaching is radically different from Judaism in the first century and the later practice of the early church – both continued to affirm the use of oaths.[2] Since it is unlikely that the Gospel writers would invent something so dissimilar from Jewish and Christian culture, this teaching is regarded as authentic. The criterion of dissimilarity therefore affirms this aspect of Jesus' teaching. It has positive force.

The distinction between positive (confirming) and negative (disproving) force should be held in mind when thinking about the other criteria as well. 'Their presence favours historicity,' says the late, great Professor Ben F. Meyer of McMaster University in Canada, 'but their absence does not of itself imply a verdict of non-historicity.'[3]

The criterion of date

The criterion of date says that early sources are preferable to later ones. The logic is simple. The less time there is between an event and its written description, the less the margin for error – for forgetting or adding. So, even with a due respect for ancient oral tradition, historians tend to favour earlier sources over later. For example, they usually give greater weight to something in the Gospel of Mark (probably written shortly before AD 70) than to the Gospel of John (probably written in the AD 90s).

The criterion of multiple attestation

Equally important is the criterion of multiple attestation. This is a technical description for a test we use on a daily basis. When you

It would be wrong to think that a later text is *necessarily* unreliable. I have already observed that Tacitus wrote his account of Tiberius almost eighty years after the emperor's death in AD 37. To offer a Jewish example, the first mention of the famed first-century rabbi known as Hillel the Elder is found in the Mishnah (AD 200), written almost two centuries after his death. Yet few contemporary scholars would deny that this text contains at least some authentic historical information about the man. And while the Gospel of John is the latest of the four Gospels, it contains unusually precise historical information. For example, I previously mentioned that the Gospel of John refers in passing to a public pool in Jerusalem 'near the Sheep Gate' which 'is called Bethesda and which is surrounded by five covered colonnades' (John 5:2). On the normal scholarly assumption the Gospel of John was written more than two decades after the destruction of Jerusalem by the Romans in AD 70, and yet this very striking description of a bathing pool in the Holy City has proved to be accurate. The late date of this source has not affected its ability to provide reliable information. Late does not automatically mean doubtful. The preference of scholars for earlier sources is perfectly valid – and, indeed, a backbone of historical inquiry – but it is not to be overplayed.

hear surprising news from one friend, you may or may not believe it. It really depends on how strange the news is and how trustworthy your friend is. But what if you heard the same news from three or four different sources – a friend, the radio, an email, a family member – and you knew they had not colluded with one another? You would almost certainly be more inclined to accept the testimony.

There are two important elements in this criterion. First, the news has to be reported in more than one source (obviously). Secondly, the sources must be *independent* of one another – that is, they cannot have been copied from one another. In the above example, it is possible that your friend, the radio and your family member all inadvertently received the news from the same hoax email. In that case, their reporting is simply *repetition*, not multiple attestation. The surest way to distinguish between these is to compare how similar the reports are. When people simply repeat news from a single source (a hoax email, for example), the words used are nearly identical. We see this when we compare newspaper reports based on the same press release – key phrases and whole sentences are simply lifted from the press release into the 'report'. However, when the same basic facts are described in very different ways, we can be fairly confident that we are dealing with multiple attestation, two or three *independent* reports of the same event. And when numerous independent sources say roughly the same thing about an event or person from the past you have a fundamental building block of historical inquiry.

Police use a similar test in assessing the testimony of those under investigation. When the 'story' of witnesses sounds just too neat, investigators often suspect collusion. But when the accounts contain real variations (while agreeing on fundamentals) this often indicates sincere, independent testimony. The New Testament contains examples of both *simple repetition* and *independent reporting*. When Matthew or Luke copy a story from Mark, this is repetition, not multiple attestation. However, when Mark and John contain a similar story, this is independent reporting, since it is generally accepted that each of these two Gospels was written without the knowledge of the other. An example will help clarify this essential historical criterion.

In his popular treatment of the life of Jesus, Episcopalian bishop and theologian John Shelby Spong suggests that the Gospels' mention of twelve apostles is spurious. Since the number of the tribes of ancient Israel was twelve, Spong writes, 'the twelve [apostles] are more symbolically real than they are actually real'.[4] Overwhelmingly, however, modern scholars accept the historicity of the twelve apostles.[5] Part of the reason is the observation that Jewish prophet figures like Jesus were well known for devising dramatic public symbols of their message.[6] More importantly, the twelve apostles is one of the most solidly attested features of the Jesus story. The Twelve are mentioned in Mark, Q, L, John and Paul – all independent sources.[7] One of these sources is very early. In 1 Corinthians 15:3–5 Paul quotes the creed (discussed earlier) which he himself had received either at his conversion in Damascus in AD 31/32 or two years later in Jerusalem (33/34). The relevant part of the creed states: 'He [Jesus] appeared to Cephas/Peter, and then to the Twelve.' This proves that by the early 30s the core group of a dozen disciples were so well known they were designated simply as 'the Twelve' and were already part of a widely publicised Christian creed.[8] In other words, in this case two important criteria – multiple attestation and early date – support the existence of Jesus' twelve apostles. The criteria of historicity often work in this mutually supportive way.

This stained glass window at Saint-Honoré d'Eylau Church in Paris, France, depicts Jesus and his disciples at the Last Supper.

The criterion of embarrassment

The criterion of embarrassment says that an episode in the Gospels that would have caused embarrassment to the early Christians (but is nonetheless reported) is unlikely to have been invented, since

Were there really twelve apostles?

The criterion of embarrassment further strengthens the historicity of the twelve apostles. It is a brute and embarrassing fact that one of the Twelve, Judas Iscariot, ended up betraying Jesus. If the Twelve were a later invention designed to symbolize the renewal of the twelve tribes of Israel (as John Shelby Spong has proposed), why on earth would a traitor be included in the story, thereby crippling the symbolism? This observation alone was sufficient to convince Professor James Charlesworth, to change his mind on the question. He had previously doubted the Gospels' lists of twelve apostles. 'The major issue concerns Judas,' he now writes. 'If "the twelve" derives only from the followers of Jesus, then it must follow that they wanted Judas to be one of the twelve. That conclusion is preposterous.'[1] Unless we are to think that the first Christians deliberately invented such evidence against interest we must conclude with Professor Ben Meyer of McMaster University that the existence of the Twelve is 'beyond reasonable doubt'.[2]

people tend not to portray themselves and their leaders in a poor light in their official histories. Lawyers call this 'evidence against interest', and they likewise regard it as a key test of truth-telling. The most obvious example is the death of Jesus. The claim that the Messiah ended up on a shameful Roman cross would have been (and was) absurd to many in the ancient world. Thus, even without the confirmation provided by Tacitus and Josephus, contemporary scholars would not for a moment doubt the embarrassing Gospel narrative about the Messiah's crucifixion. Professors Gerd Theissen and Annette Merz of Heidelberg put it bluntly: 'The execution was offensive for any worship of Jesus. As a "scandal" it cannot have been invented.'[9]

The apostle Peter's denial of Jesus during his trial provides another example of the criterion of embarrassment:

When the servant girl saw him there, she said again to those standing around, 'This fellow is one of them.' Again he denied it.

After a little while, those standing near said to Peter, 'Surely you are one of them, for you are a Galilean.'

He began to call down curses, and he swore to them, 'I don't know this man you're talking about.'

Immediately the rooster crowed the second time. Then Peter remembered the word Jesus had spoken to him: 'Before the rooster crows twice you will disown me three times.' And he broke down and wept.

Mark 14:69–72

Peter was so revered in the early church – the church that produced the New Testament – that it is very unlikely the Gospel writers would have included a story like this unless it just happened to be

(embarrassingly) true. This point is intensified when we remember (as explained at the beginning of Chapter 8) that the Gospel of Mark records the eyewitness testimony of Peter himself.

Another feature of the Jesus story supported by the criterion of embarrassment is the role of the female disciples as witnesses to the empty tomb and resurrection. Surprisingly, all four Gospels tell how the women followers of Jesus were the first to learn that the tomb in which Jesus had been laid was empty and that he was alive. Leaving to one side the question of the resurrection itself, most scholars find it striking that these first-century texts would give such a prominent role to women, especially given that the testimony of women was

The Denial of Saint Peter (c. 1620–1625), by Gerard Seghers.

considered suspect in antiquity. Consider the following passage from John's Gospel:

Early on the first day of the week, while it was still dark, Mary Magdalene went to the tomb and saw that the stone had been removed from the entrance …

At this, she turned around and saw Jesus standing there, but she did not realize that it was Jesus.

He asked her, 'Woman, why are you crying? Who is it you are looking for?'

A garden tomb, similar to that of Jesus.

Thinking he was the gardener, she said, 'Sir, if you have carried him away, tell me where you have put him, and I will get him.'

Jesus said to her, 'Mary.'

She turned toward him and cried out in Aramaic, 'Rabboni!' (which means 'Teacher').

Jesus said, 'Do not hold on to me, for I have not yet ascended to the Father. Go instead to my brothers and tell them, "I am ascending to my Father and your Father, to my God and your God."'

Mary Magdalene went to the disciples with the news: 'I have seen the Lord!' And she told them that he had said these things to her.

John 20:1–18; see also Mark 16:1–8; Matthew 28:1–8; Luke 24:1–12, 22–23

The presence of women in the story of Jesus' resurrection is 'one of the firmest features of the tradition in all its variation', writes Professor James Dunn. However, 'as is well known, in Middle Eastern society of the time women were not regarded as reliable witnesses: a woman's testimony in court was heavily discounted'.[10] Two ancient Jewish texts underline this point. Josephus writes: 'From women let no evidence be accepted, because of the levity and temerity of their sex.'[11] A similar outlook can be observed in the ancient Jewish law book called the Mishnah: 'The law governing an oath of testimony applies to men and not to women, to those who are suitable to bear witness and not to those who are unsuitable to bear witness.'[12]

The significance of the observation is clear. Unless it was well

The Holy Women at the Tomb, by Ridolfo Ghirlandaio (1483–1561).

known from the beginning that women were the first to find an empty tomb, why would all four Gospel report it? The writers of the New Testament 'were well aware of customary attitudes to the testimony of women', writes Professor Graham Stanton, 'but they simply recorded the traditions they received, even though they would have carried little weight in arguments with opponents.'[13] Put simply, unless it were simply (and embarrassingly) true that women were the first to make these claims, the Gospel writers are unlikely to have narrated such a story.[14]

Again, the criterion of embarrassment can only be applied positively, as in the above examples. It cannot be used *negatively,* that is, to disprove parts of the Gospels, since obviously not everything Jesus said or did would have been embarrassing to his followers.

Once these criteria of dissimilarity, date, multiple attestation and embarrassment are employed, a fairly large base of data about Jesus begins to emerge. Other methods used by historians shape these data into a coherent whole, providing us with a historically plausible portrait of the man from Nazareth. These further tests are discussed in the final chapter.

10

CHAPTER

Assessing Historical Plausibility

Historians are not content simply to find 'data' about Jesus – a random list of things he probably said and did. True history fleshes out data into a coherent and factual whole.[1] It is about creating a portrait of an event or person from the past that fits into its broader context. There are various methods and principles which assist this project. What follows is only a small selection of a wide variety.

The criterion of coherence

The criterion of coherence ('holding together') comes into play only after the criteria of dissimilarity, multiple attestation and embarrassment have produced some solid results. Once historians have established some basic 'facts', they can look at other material in the Gospels, which may not be so well attested, and ask: Does this cohere with what we already know about Jesus? This is called the criterion of coherence. Professor John P. Meier puts it this way: 'Other sayings and deeds of Jesus that fit in well with the preliminary "data base" established by using our first three criteria have a good chance of being historical.'[2] Let me offer an example.

It is certain in the opinion of virtually all experts that Jesus preached about the arrival of a divine kingdom in which God would overthrow evil, establish justice and restore the creation itself. He called this 'the kingdom of God'. Clear statements about this kingdom are found in a range of independent sources in the New Testament: multiple attestation, in other words, confirms this theme as central to his preaching. The criterion of coherence, then, can be applied to numerous other sayings of Jesus which, while not attested more than once, nevertheless fit with what we know Jesus said about the kingdom. Numerous parables about God's coming reign are regarded as authentic on these grounds, even though they appear in just one source. For example, the teaching of Jesus in the parable of the wise and foolish maidens (Matthew 25:1–13, as quoted here on page 117) appears only in the Gospel of Matthew (or his special source known as M). If this particular parable had little resonance with the more established teachings of Jesus, scholars might choose to doubt that it really came from his lips. However,

The Good Samaritan

Jesus' famous parable of the Good Samaritan is an example of teaching that coheres well with the rest of what Jesus taught. It appears only in the Gospel of Luke (probably from his special source, L):

'A man was going down from Jerusalem to Jericho, when he fell into the hands of robbers. They stripped him of his clothes, beat him and went away, leaving him half dead. A priest happened to be going down the same road, and when he saw the man, he passed by on the other side. So too, a Levite, when he came to the place and saw him, passed by on the other side. But a Samaritan, as he travelled, came where the man was; and when he saw him, he took pity on him. He went to him and bandaged his wounds, pouring on oil and wine. Then he put the man on his own donkey, brought him to an inn and took care of him. The next day he took out two silver coins and gave them to the innkeeper. "Look after him," he said, "and when I return, I will reimburse you for any extra expense you may have."

'Which of these three do you think was a neighbour to the man who fell into the hands of robbers?'
Luke 10:30–36

It is possible that Luke simply created this parable. However, 'it coheres with what has already been proved to be reliable traditions from Jesus', writes the historian Professor James Charlesworth of Princeton Theological Seminary. It 'fits perfectly the emphasis on pollution and purity, which was a hallmark of pre-70 Palestinian Jews living not only in Judea but in Lower Galilee. Finally, it is coherent with Jesus' inclusion of the marginalized.'[1]

the reference to the kingdom of God and the emphasis on urgency in this parable – themes frequently observed in Jesus' 'authentic' teachings – reassure scholars. This teaching coheres well with what we know Jesus taught. It is thus regarded as probably authentic.

Obviously, this criterion cannot be applied negatively, since, as Professor John P.

The Parable of the Good Samaritan, an illustration from the mid-nineteenth century book, *Christian Doctrine for Families*.

Meier points out: 'Jesus would hardly be unique among the great thinkers or leaders of world history if his sayings and actions did not always seem totally consistent to us.'[3] The criterion of coherence *rules in* many of Jesus' sayings and deeds, but only with difficulty can it rule any out.

The criterion of historical plausibility

The criterion of historical plausibility states that when an episode or teaching in the Gospels clearly reflects an early Palestinian Jewish setting the likelihood of it being authentic is increased (this is sometimes also called the criterion of Palestinian Jewish setting). The logic is compelling. The Gospels were written in Greek, outside the Holy Land and (with the exception of Mark) after the year AD 70, when Jerusalem and its Temple were destroyed. The temptation for the Gospel writers would surely have been to make their stories more relevant to their respective Greco-Roman settings, whether Rome, Ephesus or Syria. Given this, material in the Gospels with peculiar resonance to a pre-AD 70 Jewish Palestinian setting is unlikely to have been invented. 'When a Palestinian Jewish setting is discerned in a passage,' writes James Charlesworth, 'then it represents Jesus' time and place and not the Evangelist's time or place.'[4] Charlesworth himself offers the example of the woman caught in adultery who was brought to Jesus in the Jerusalem Temple:

> *At dawn he appeared again in the temple courts, where all the people gathered around him, and he sat down to teach them. The teachers of the law and the Pharisees brought in a woman caught in adultery. They made her stand before the group and said to Jesus, 'Teacher, this woman was caught in the act of adultery. In the Law Moses commanded us to stone such women. Now what do you say?' They were using this question as a trap, in order to have a basis for accusing him.*
>
> *But Jesus bent down and started to write on the ground with his finger. When they kept on questioning him, he straightened up and said to them, 'Let any one of you who is without sin be the first to throw a stone at her.' Again he stooped down and wrote on the ground.*
>
> *At this, those who heard began to go away one at a time, the older ones first, until only Jesus was left, with the woman still standing there. Jesus straightened up and asked her, 'Woman, where are they? Has no one condemned you?'*
>
> *'No one, sir,' she said.*
>
> *'Then neither do I condemn you,' Jesus declared. 'Go now and leave your life of sin.'*
> **John 8:2–11**

Most English Bibles note in the margins that this story does not appear in the earliest manuscripts of John's Gospel. In the opinion of most scholars, it was never part of the original Gospel. But this does not mean the story is untrue. Many experts believe that this was in fact an authentic episode from Jesus' life that was retained in oral tradition until some time in the second century, when it was inserted into some manuscripts of the Gospel of John. The historical plausibility of the story is clear, as Charlesworth notes: 'It fits into Jesus' Jewish environment (the setting is a realistic depiction of the time when the Temple was the center of worship). It accurately preserves the tension over oral legislation between Jesus and some scribes and Pharisees.'[5]

At this point it is important to acknowledge the many background sources historians use to gain a picture of what is plausible in the story of Jesus. Historical figures have to be placed in their particular cultural context. Otherwise, we will end up studying characters in a vacuum or, worse, importing our own

Christ and the Woman Taken in Adultery, c. 1540, by Lucas Cranach the Elder.

Ritual baths and vessels

Evidence of a pre-AD 70 Palestinian Jewish setting in the Gospels includes the references to ritual baths and ritual stone containers. In John 2:6 passing reference is made to 'six stone water jars, the kind used by the Jews for ceremonial washing'. In John 9 Jesus urges a man to wash himself in the Pool of Siloam, a large *mikveh* or ritual bath. The important thing to observe here, as Charlesworth points out, is that ritual baths and stone vessels 'characterize Jewish religious life before 70 and not after it'.[1] Indeed, until fifty years ago scholars had little evidence of how obsessed pre-AD 70 religious Jews were with sacred bathing and the purity of their containers. Discoveries at Qumran and in Jerusalem brought all this to light only in the 1950s. The Gospels made this plain from the very beginning.

twenty-first-century assumptions into first-century texts. Scholars of the historical Jesus therefore study as much as they can about the geography, politics, architecture, leisure and writings of the period. These form the backdrop, the canvas, on which all plausible portraits of the man from Nazareth must be sketched. The list of background sources from the period is enormous: on the Jewish side there are the Dead Sea Scrolls, Philo, Josephus, the Pseudepigrapha and the Mishnah; on the Greco-Roman side we have Seneca, Plutarch, Tacitus, Pliny and Suetonius (just to name a few). Two examples will suffice to show the importance of these background sources for determining plausibility in the life of Jesus.

One cannot read the Gospels without being struck by the constant scandal Jesus causes by his associations with the so-called 'sinners'. After

An example of the *mikveh*, the ritual bath, in the ruins of the ancient Essene settlement of Qumran.

2,000 years of Christianization it now seems perfectly reasonable that one is to love even the immoral and irreligious. Our sources tell a different story. In a collection of writings known as the Pseudepigrapha, we find a text called the *Psalms of Solomon*. It was penned by a Jewish leader probably in Jerusalem around 50 BC. It offers a clear picture of the hatred that existed towards 'sinners':[6]

> *The sinner stumbles and curses his life,*
> *the day of his birth, and his mother's pains.*
> *He adds sin upon sin in his life;*
> *he falls – his fall is serious – and he will not get up.*
> *The destruction of the sinner is forever,*
> *and he will not be remembered when God looks after the*
> *righteous.*
> *This is the share of the sinners forever.*
> **Psalms of Solomon 3:9–12**

> *But they [the righteous] shall pursue sinners and overtake*
> *them,*
> *for those who act lawlessly shall not escape the Lord's*
> *judgment.*
> *They shall be overtaken as by those experienced in war,*
> *for on their forehead is the mark of destruction.*
> *And the inheritance of sinners is destruction*
> *and darkness.*
> **Psalms of Solomon 15:8–9**

Suddenly, Jesus' meals with the immoral and the scandal they caused, according to the Gospels, can be viewed in a plausible light.

Some teachings of Jesus are clearly understood only in the light of what we now know of debates among pre-AD 70 Jews concerning the Sabbath. According to one text in Matthew's Gospel, Jesus taught: 'If any of you has a sheep and it falls into a pit on the Sabbath, will you not take hold of it and lift it out? How much more valuable is a human

The Psalms of Solomon, housed in the John Rylands Library, Manchester, UK.

being than a sheep! Therefore it is lawful to do good on the Sabbath' (Matthew 12:11–12). The discovery of the so called *Damascus Document* in the Dead Sea Scrolls has shown Jesus' example to be part of a real debate among Jews of the period – something which sounds amazing to us now. The text reads: 'No-one should help an animal give birth on the Sabbath day. And if it falls into a well or a pit, he should not take it out on the Sabbath … And any living man who falls into a place of water or into a reservoir (on the Sabbath), no-one should take him out with a ladder or a rope or a utensil.'[7] As Professor James Charlesworth, the Director of the Princeton Dead Sea Scrolls Project, writes: 'The link between Jesus' teaching and the Essene injunction is at once impressive and astounding.'[8]

Examples of the importance of the background sources for discerning the plausibility of Jesus' teaching could be offered *ad infinitum*. Jewish and Greco-Roman writings alike bring a rich colour to the Gospels and confirm that the figure at the heart of these texts is no late invention but a flesh-and-blood Jew of the first half of the first century.

The criterion of archaic language

Other indications of a Palestinian Jewish setting (and therefore of historical plausibility) include the numerous examples of Aramaic language in the Gospels. The Gospels were composed in Greek, and yet we know that Jesus spoke Aramaic, the language of Palestine in the period (he may also have taught in Hebrew). Numerous Aramaic experts have tried taking the sayings of Jesus (in our Greek Gospels) and 'retroverted' them into first century Aramaic. The result is a 'new poetic force and even greater clarity of meaning', says Professor John P. Meier.[9] For instance, in the Lord's Prayer, Jesus taught his disciples to pray: 'And forgive us our debts, as we also have forgiven our debtors' (Matthew 6:12).[10] The word 'debt' is not a typical Greek or Hebrew way of speaking about wrongdoing. However, the Aramaic noun for 'debt', hoba, is often used with this metaphorical meaning,[11] suggesting that the Gospels have preserved for us something belonging to Jesus' specific cultural context. This line of reasoning is called the *criterion of archaic language*; it may be thought of as a subset of the *criterion of historical plausibility*.

On occasion the Gospel writers do not even bother to remove certain Aramaic words. In Mark 14:36 we are told of the anguished prayer Jesus uttered in the moments before his arrest: '*Abba*, Father,' he said, 'everything is possible for you. Take this cup from me. Yet not what I will, but what you will.' The strange thing here is that Mark actually writes out in Greek script the Aramaic way of saying 'father', *abba*. He literally pens the letters *alpha beta beta alpha* – which has no meaning in Greek – and then he adds the Greek translation *pater*, 'father'. Most scholars think that '*abba*/ father' was such a conspicuous feature of Jesus' way of talking about God (in Aramaic) that even the Greek-speaking Christians carried over this word into their own vocabulary.[12]

Finally, in a passage from Matthew's special source (M), Jesus insults the Pharisees in a way that can only be fully appreciated

The author views the Dead Sea Scrolls at the Shrine of the Book Museum in Jerusalem, Israel.

against a Palestinian Aramaic background: 'You blind guides! You strain out a gnat but swallow a camel' (Matthew 23:24). In Aramaic 'gnat' is *qalma* and 'camel' is *gamla*. This poetic wordplay, known as paronomasia, is lost in the Greek of the Gospels, but, once recovered, surely indicates that Matthew has reported an old oral tradition about Jesus.

It hardly needs to be said by now that while the presence of such archaic (Aramaic) language in the Gospels indicates good historical tradition, its absence does not suggest the opposite. The fact that a teaching of Jesus appears in the Gospels in very good Greek, without any hint of its Aramaic origin, does not mean it came from the Gospel writer rather than Jesus. We now know that Greek was quite widely spoken in Jerusalem in Jesus' day. His sayings could have been transposed into good Greek even within his lifetime. Let me explain.

Throughout the *western* part of the Mediterranean (anything to the 'left' of Palestine) the common language was Greek.[13] Large communities of Jews also spoke Greek, not only in Rome, Corinth and Alexandria but also in Palestine itself. Professor Martin Hengel, among others, has demonstrated just how prevalent the Greek language was in Jerusalem, even among Jews.[14] It is estimated that as much as 15 per cent of the population of the city spoke Greek as their main language.[15] Entire Greek-speaking synagogues are known to have existed in the Holy City, and at least two of Jesus' own disciples (Philip and Andrew)

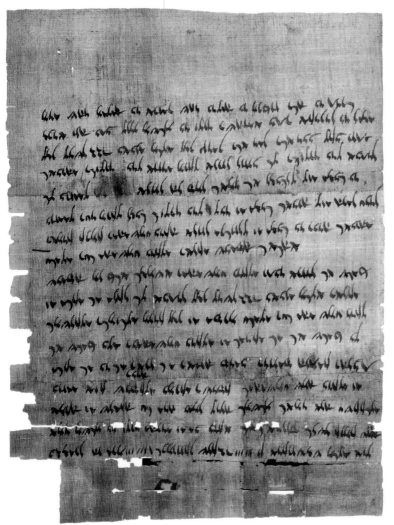

Freedom for Tamut and Yehoishem, an Aramaic document dated 3 July 449 BC. It was discovered on Elephantine Island, Egypt.

bore distinctly Greek names, suggesting they themselves spoke the language.[16] Moreover, while Jesus' first language was undoubtedly Aramaic, his trade as a carpenter would have given him ample opportunity to learn what John P. Meier describes as 'practical, business type' Greek,[17] just enough to engage commercially with the many Greek-speakers in Palestine. Other scholars, such as the Australian New Testament historian Paul Barnett, even believe that 'on occasion Jesus conversed and taught in Greek'.[18]

The criterion of memorability

The criterion of memorability suggests that teachings of Jesus which are inherently memorable are more likely to have been remembered accurately in oral tradition and therefore recorded correctly in the later Gospels.

Some of Jesus' sayings were memorable for their simple drama: 'If your right eye causes you to stumble, gouge it out and throw it away. It is better for you to lose one part of your body than for your

View of modern-day Jerusalem.

The gospel in Greek

It is probable that Jesus' teaching was being retold in Greek almost immediately after his death. We know that soon after AD 30 the Christian community in Jerusalem was made up of two distinct groups: those whose main language was Aramaic and those whose main language was Greek.[1] The Aramaic group is easy to explain – this was the vast majority of those who followed him. But where did the Greek-speaking group come from so soon? There are two explanations. Either Jesus himself had some influence on Greek-speaking Jews or else, more likely, some of his first, bilingual disciples (perhaps Philip and Andrew) enjoyed rapid success in converting Greek-speaking Jews to the faith. Whichever was the case, the point is significant for historical studies. What we have in the Greek Gospels is not a late, foreign rendition of a much earlier Aramaic (and therefore different) story of Jesus. It is now perfectly clear that the Aramaic stories and teachings of Jesus were recast into the Greek language while many of the eyewitnesses, some of whom spoke fluent Greek themselves, still remained in Jerusalem.[2]

whole body to be thrown into hell' (Matthew 5:29). This is a classic example of Jewish hyperbole. Once heard, it is unlikely ever to be forgotten.

Other teachings of Jesus were *designed* for memorization. They contain 'mnemonic' devices, such as rhyme, rhythm, alliteration and parallelism, which aid the disciple to recall and pass on the teaching.[19] This was a very common method in ancient cultures. When only a small section of the population could read, important traditions were best preserved not in writing – which was accessible only to a few – but by hearing, repeating and memorizing. A committed disciple would have no problem, for instance, in accurately reciting the following saying of Jesus:

'Why do you look at the speck of sawdust in someone else's eye and pay no attention to the plank in your own eye? How can you say, "Let me take the speck out of your eye," when all the time there is a plank in your own eye? You hypocrite, first take the plank out of your own eye, and then you will see clearly to remove the speck from the other person's eye.'
Matthew 7:3–5, paralleled in Luke 6:41–42

If you read the above passage through several times, you will observe a clear pattern involving parallelism, contrast, hyperbole and repetition. Once you spot the pattern, I suspect you could easily and accurately quote the paragraph to someone else. Memorization would be further enhanced if you met with others each week to rehearse such material, as the early Christians did.

The memorablility of many of Jesus' sayings does not prove that they come from Jesus. It is of course possible that later Christians invented memorable sayings and placed them on the lips of Jesus; decided sceptics still have some wriggle room. However, as I have said repeatedly, most scholars do not come to the New Testament with sceptical prejudice determined to reject what cannot be proven beyond doubt. Instead, they begin with the assumption that the Gospel writers were ultimately 'traditionalists', concerned to *preserve* more than to innovate (Luke's and Matthew's use of Mark and Q prove this). When a saying such as the one above is found only in one source – in this case in Q – historians do not reject it outright. They ask questions such as: How well does it fit with what we already know of Jesus? (the criterion of coherence); and, How likely is it that a saying like this would be preserved accurately between AD 30 (when Jesus died) and AD 50 (when Q was probably written)? In the above case, both questions receive a positive answer.

The memorability of the stories of Jesus

Memorability is a feature not only of many of Jesus' sayings but also of the accounts of his actions. It has long been observed that the sparse, patterned and self-contained way the individual stories of Jesus are told in the Gospels was highly conducive to memorization. Consider the following story and notice how extraneous details are conspicuous by their absence in what must have been a very dramatic and tense event:

> *On reaching Jerusalem, Jesus entered the temple courts and began driving out those who were buying and selling there. He overturned the tables of the money changers and the benches of those selling doves, and would not allow anyone to carry merchandise through the temple courts. And as he taught them, he said, 'Is it not written: "My house will be called a house of prayer for all nations"? But you have made it "a den of robbers".'*
> *The chief priests and the teachers of the law heard this and began looking for a way to kill him, for they feared him, because the whole crowd was amazed at his teaching.*
> **Mark 11:15–18**

This is typical of the no-nonsense, bare minimum storytelling of the Gospels (the crucifixion narratives show even greater restraint). Only the core elements of the event are included, even though this was a significant moment in the narrative – ultimately leading to Jesus' arrest and execution. It would have easily lent itself to literary elaboration if that had been part of the author's intention.

Why are so many Gospel episodes like this? It was once thought that the final form of these stories was the result of a slow process of evolution, as Christian communities honed and edited the material for ongoing remembrance and relevance. But this perspective has been dealt some strong blows in recent years, not least from Professor James Dunn of Durham University and Professor Richard Bauckham of the University of St Andrew's. Dunn has shown that oral tradition did not work on an evolutionary model where each new 'performance' built on the previous one until the final form – the one in the Gospels – can be thought of as the most highly developed. Instead, oral tradition always displayed a combination of fixity and flexibility. The core details remained the same but each new performance could adapt the story to the particular situation. On this model the twenty-third performance of a story cannot be thought of as any less authentic than the third retelling – much in the same way as a modern joke can be retold with some variation without actually evolving in a linear way. The version of the story of Jesus' entry into Jerusalem, which ended up being written down by Mark in the 60s AD, is probably no more or less 'developed' than the version that was being told in the 30s AD.[20]

Richard Bauckham has taken Dunn's insights further, and

The Temple built by Herod the Great stands in the forefront in this model of first-century Jerusalem.

with a subtle critique. He shows that the stories about Jesus were preserved not just by anonymous communities but by individual eyewitnesses who were recognized as the overseers and guardians of the oral traditions. We catch a glimpse of this role in the opening statement of Luke's Gospel: 'those who from the first were eyewitnesses and servants of the word' (Luke 1:2). If the Christian community was the orchestra rehearsing the stories of Jesus over and over, these authorized 'servants of the word' were the conductors ensuring that the material was being faithfully remembered and performed.[21] In passage after passage throughout the New Testament we find evidence that authoritative individuals, not just churches in general, were responsible for protecting the traditions about Jesus.[22] This is the context in which we are to understand the sparse, patterned and self-contained manner in which the Gospel stories are told. From the very beginning, official witnesses and Christian communities retained and retold the stories in a way that would aid their verbal transmission.

Archaeology

While not a criterion in the strict sense, archaeology plays an increasingly important role in probing the historical character of the story of Jesus. In the last decade some very significant information has been uncovered throughout Israel. This has given us fresh eyes for reading the Gospels – though 'fresh' is probably not the right word, since what the archaeology provides is a way to read the story as ancient people would have.[23]

Sometimes archaeology accidentally confirms incidental details of the Gospels. In Chapter 3 I discussed the excavations in Jerusalem between 1957 and 1962 which uncovered the five-colonnade pool mentioned in John 5:2, a pool whose existence some scholars doubted. John 9:7 mentions a second bathing pool in another part of Jerusalem: '"Go" [Jesus told a blind man], "wash in the Pool of Siloam" (this word means "Sent"). So the man went and washed, and came home seeing.' This pool had eluded scholars for decades. A 'Pool of Siloam' dating from the Byzantine period had been uncovered but not one from the time of Jesus. Then, in June 2004, during sewerage repairs in the Siloam district of Jerusalem,

Richard Bauckham has brought new depth to the idea of verbal transmission of memories by appealing to modern psychological studies of recollective memory. In a wide-ranging chapter in his *Jesus and the Eyewitnesses* he draws attention to the fact that memories are frequently retold in a schematized way, that is, in a fashion easily digestible (and repeatable) in the particular cultural context. Key to this schematization is the removal of extraneous details so as to give the story a more straightforward and memorable shape. Perhaps most significant is the fact that this process occurs very quickly. The first few retellings of a memory, according to the evidence, tend to fix the form of all future renditions.[1] (Readers will no doubt have numerous personal examples of stories – of a school prank, a wedding day, a sporting victory and so on – which are retold in much the same way as they have been for years.) The significance of Bauckham's research for the study of Jesus is clear. The economical, ordered and memorable shape of many of the stories in the Gospels is not the result of a long evolutionary process of community honing, but a function of the way in which the first witnesses rapidly schematized their retellings of Jesus' life, so as to encourage the wide and faithful transmission of the story through oral tradition.

workers accidentally uncovered a huge public bath, the largest of its type ever found. The news was announced to the world in three articles in the *Jerusalem Post*: 10 June 2004, page 5; 25 June 2004, page 12; 24 December 2004, page 6. Coins in and around the pool confirm that it was in public use between the first century BC and AD 70. It is without doubt the pool mentioned by John [24] I have visited the pool twice now, and each time excavations reveal more and more about the pool and its surrounding area.

Archaeology does more than just occasionally confirm incidental details of the Gospels. Sometimes it has power to overturn entire scholarly theories about Jesus. From 1988 to the mid-1990s some scholars argued that Jesus was not as deeply Jewish as the Gospels portray him, but rather was shaped by

Painting of the pool of Siloam.

his Greco-Roman environment and by the philosophy of the Cynics in particular.[25] Some vague parallels between Jesus' teaching and practice and that of the Cynics were brought forward, but the theory was also heavily dependent on the fact that remains of towns in Lower Galilee looked pagan in style. With this starting point, these scholars started to remove from the Gospels many of the things that sound overtly Jewish: Jesus' disputes over the Jewish law, his emphasis on the 'kingdom of God', his call to repentance, his allusions to the Old Testament and so on. It was argued that these elements were added to the original Jesus story by the Gospel writers. In other words, the Gospels had 'Judaized' a Jesus who was originally a kind of wandering Cynic philosopher. This was a major starting point for the so-called Jesus Seminar, a small group of scholars, mainly in the United States, determined to uncover the 'true Jesus'.

A Jewish ossuary box.

The Jesus Seminar has been quiet in the last few years because archaeological investigations have posed serious problems for the theory. The Galilee that scholars have continued to uncover is only *superficially* pagan – in architecture. In terms of the deep material culture, that is, the physical markers of a people, it is unmistakably Jewish. The four great archaeological signs of Jewish society are ritual baths known as *mikvaot*, bowls made of limestone, special burial practices and the absence of pig bones. Lower Galilee has all of these signs in striking regularity. It is now certain that Jesus' cultural influences growing up were intensely Jewish. Archaeology has debunked an entire theory and shown the Gospels' portrait of a very Jewish Galilean to be historically sound.[26]

No scholar believes that archaeological discoveries like these, or the application of the historical criteria outlined above, provide a flawless path to the truth, the whole truth and nothing but the truth about Jesus. History is not an exact science, and a margin for error definitely exists. Nevertheless, readers should also be aware that the considerations discussed in the last two chapters lead most experts working in the field today to accept that the *core* of the Gospel story is both plausible and probable. Few, if any, experts in

the historical Jesus approach the New Testament as God's infallible Word – a Christian doctrine that must be argued on philosophical rather than historical grounds – but almost all of them would agree with the conclusion of Professor Graham Stanton of Cambridge University: 'While certainty often eludes us, we do know a good deal about Jesus of Nazareth.'[27] In closing I will say something about what the historian means by 'knowing' something about the past.

Ruins of the synagogue at Arbel.

Conclusion:
Probability and Proof

Despite the seriousness with which historians grapple with the various sources and methods described in this book, it has to be said that no one thinks we possess proof positive for the sayings or deeds of Jesus. Unlike mathematical or scientific 'facts' which can often be proved or disproved, historical facts have to do with degrees of probability. However, that does not make history a second-class type of knowledge. This has to be said over and over again today because with the laudable success of the sciences has come an overreaching confidence among some about what constitutes real knowledge. For some, the only true knowledge is scientific knowledge.

But philosophers, to whom scientists and historians alike should listen on such matters, often point out that the areas of knowledge where science speaks with authority are limited – and the same is true for history, of course.[1] Science usually trades in the repeatable and observable. It repeats tests of the effects of certain chemicals on the human body; it observes the 'background waves' of a cosmic explosion 13.7 billion years ago. Within the sphere of the repeatable and observable the scientific method works brilliantly.

However, we cannot demand a scientific form of evidence for events that are unrepeatable and unobservable. Otherwise, we would rule out virtually all historical information. Historical events are, by definition, incapable of being observed or repeated. The same logic would also rule out most legal judgments, since, unless forensic analysis is involved, courts of law operate without recourse to science; instead, they weigh testimony, scrutinize motives, assess circumstances and so on, much as historians do.

Like legal judgment, historical judgment has its own valid way of arriving at the knowledge of something. This was a point driven home years ago by the famous Oxford philosopher, historian and archaeologist R. G. Collingwood. In *The Idea of History* he argued that history is not a poor cousin of the exact sciences. It stands on its own and is uniquely qualified to discern the shape of the past. It is its own science:

> *History, then, is a science, but a science of a special kind. It is a science whose business is to study events not accessible to our observation, and to study these events inferentially, arguing to them from something else which is accessible to our observation, and which the historian calls 'evidence' for the events in which he is interested.*[2]

Everyone agrees that *absolute certainty* cannot be found in historical knowledge – so also in a court of law. But that is no problem. 'Beyond reasonable doubt' will do just fine. Many of life's most important decisions (the career we pursue, the partner we choose, the way we vote, the house or car we purchase, the way we raise our children) are made without anything like the certainty of a mathematical theorem. Even with a thorough knowledge of the original languages, an intimate understanding of the primary texts, a rigorous application of historical criteria and a deep awareness of all the relevant archaeological and cultural data, the historian will only ever be able to talk about *degrees of probability* in historical conclusions.

Historians do sometimes use the language of 'certainty'. They are perfectly comfortable, for instance, saying that Jesus' existence is certain (only the ill informed or ill motivated could say otherwise). But when they use this language they are not doing so in the way a physicist might speak of being certain of some physical constant, for example, the mass–energy equivalence formula, $E = mc^2$. Certainty in history is sometimes termed 'moral certainty'. This has nothing to do with morality. It is a reference to the integrity of evidence and reason. Some things are so plentifully

Pilate Stone at the Archaeological Park in Caesarea.

supported by the evidence that, although they can be rejected by someone determined to do so, most will agree they are beyond reasonable doubt. Most legal judgments depend on moral certainty.

An example of the historian's certainty is found in the case of Pontius Pilate. The evidence that Pilate governed southern Palestine (Judea) around the year 30 is overwhelming. The four Gospels and the New Testament book of Acts mention it, as do the Jewish writers Philo and Josephus and the great Roman historian Tacitus. Moreover, in 1961 an inscription was found on the coast of Palestine, in Caesarea Maritima, which names Pontius Pilate as 'Prefect' of Judea. Is it *absolutely* certain, therefore, that Pilate governed Palestine in the first century? No. It is not outside the realm of possibility that the manuscripts of Josephus, Philo and Tacitus have all been 'edited' by the same people who copied the New Testament and that the Pilate inscription from Caesarea is a master forgery. The whole thing *could* be a sham. It is possible. But is it reasonable to think such a thing? Of course not. Professor John P. Meier, from whom I borrowed this example, writes: 'But since any of these possibilities (not to mention all of them together) is so extremely unlikely, we are justified in considering our conclusion morally certain, especially since, in daily life, we constantly make firm theoretical judgments and practical decisions on the basis of high probability.'[3]

The point of all this is to say that 'proof' of the historical kind is really just a way of saying *very high probability*. And very high probability is usually enough in every day life to believe that I *know* something to be true. To offer an example closer to the present, I never met my maternal great-grandparents, Herbert and Ethel, who lived in the English town of St Anne's-on-Sea, owned a successful cotton mill and frequented their holiday house on the French Riviera (which, sadly, no longer remains in the family). My knowledge of these things is based entirely on family report, not firm 'proof' – I have not even seen their birth certificates. But does this mean that I am not justified in believing them to be true? Of course not. There is a very high probability that this information has been preserved accurately. And in everyday life *very high probability* is usually enough to allow us to say that we *know* something.

This is the sense in which historians of all persuasions agree that, while many doubts remain over the details, the core elements of Jesus' life are in fact *known*. Whatever those on the fringes continue to say, there is an overwhelming scholarly consensus today that a Galilean teacher and (reputed) healer named Jesus proclaimed the arrival of God's kingdom, wined and dined with 'sinners', appointed a circle of twelve apostles, clashed with religious authorities, denounced the Jerusalem Temple and wound up dead on a Roman cross; shortly after which his first followers declared they had seen him alive again, announced he was the long-awaited Messiah and sought to preserve and promote (first in oral form, then in writing) all that they could of their memorable master's life. The sources and methods contemporary scholars use allow *certainty* on at least these elements of the ancient Gospel story.

Notes

Introduction: *Jesus on the Fringe*

1. G. A. Wells, *Did Jesus Exist?*, Prometheus Books, 1975, pp. 205-7.

2. Richard Dawkins, *The God Delusion*, Bantam Press, 2006, p. 97.

3. G. W. Clarke, 'The Origins and Spread of Christianity', in *The Cambridge Ancient History, vol. X: The Augustan Empire, 43 BC–AD 69*, Cambridge University Press, 1996, pp. 848–72.

4. Email correspondence of 13 March 2008.

5. 'I am tempted to go further and wonder in what possible sense theologians can be said to have a province.' Dawkins, *The God Delusion*, p. 56.

6. E. P. Sanders, *The Historical Figure of Jesus*, Penguin Books, 1993, p. 11.

7. Christopher Hitchens, *God is not Great: How Religion Poisons Everything*, Twelve, 2007, pp. 114.

8. Michel Onfray, *The Atheist Manifesto*, Arcade Publishing, 2005, pp. 115–16.

1   The Quest for Jesus from Beginnings to the Enlightenment

1. Richard Bauckham, *Jesus and the Eyewitnesses: The Gospels as Eyewitness Testimony*, Eerdmans, 2006, pp. 114–54 (though the entire book is worth reading on this score).

2. The full interview may be found on *The Christ Files* DVD, Blue Bottle Books, 2008.

3. As we will see, it was David Friedrich Strauss who first proposed the spiritual or 'mythical' reading of the Gospels more than 170 years ago (in his 1835/6 work *The Life of Jesus Critically Examined*). Despite initial excitement, the theory was all but dead in scholarship by the early 1900s. Popular authors like Bishop John Shelby Spong are unwitting heirs of Strauss.

4. Eusebius, the fourth-century bishop of Caesarea (on the coast of modern Israel), wrote: 'Many of those then disciples … took up the work of evangelists and were zealous to preach to all who had not yet heard the word of the faith, and to transmit the writing of the divine Gospels.'

Eusebius, *Ecclesiastical History 3.37.2*.

5. Here I am indebted to the excellent account of Origen's contribution to biblical scholarship in David Dungan's *A History of the Synoptic Problem*, Doubleday, 1999, pp. 65–88.

6. In about AD 170 Tatian of Rome had attempted to harmonize the four Gospels into a single, unproblematic account of Jesus' life. It was called the *Diatessaron*, Greek for 'through the four [Gospels]'. It is a tribute to the early church that the majority rejected this easy option, preferring to wrestle with the four different accounts of Christ we still find in our New Testaments.

7. Nicholas Wolterstorff, *Reason within the Bounds of Religion*, 2nd edition, Eerdmans, 1999.

8. Deism began in the mid to late 1600s with English writers such as Lord Edward Herbert of Cherbury (1583–1648), John Toland (1670–1722), Thomas Woolston (1670–1733) and Lord Anthony Ashley Cooper, Earl of Shaftesbury (1671–1713). Deism insisted that worship of a largely unknown Creator was just about the only religious 'truth' accessible to human reason. All other doctrines were speculative accumulations born of humanity's innate religious instinct.

9. Reimarus, *Fragments*, edited by C. H. Talbert, Fortress Press, 1971.

10. A modern English edition is David Friedrich Strauss, *The Life of Jesus Critically Examined*, SCM, 1973.

11. John Shelby Spong, *Jesus for the Non-Religious*, HarperCollins, 2007.

12. The first English edition was Ernest Renan, *The Life of Jesus*, Trubner, 1864.

13. The English edition is William Wrede, *The Messianic Secret*, James Clarke, 1971.

14. Wrede pointed to passages such as Romans 1:4 and Acts 2:32–36.

15. N. T. Wright, 'Quest for the Historical Jesus', in *The Anchor Bible Dictionary*, vol. III, Doubleday, 1992, p. 797.

16. The most recent English edition of this 1906 German classic is Albert Schweitzer, *The Quest of the Historical Jesus*, Dover, 2005.

17. The original German title was *Von Reimarus zu Wrede*.

18. Schweitzer, *The Quest of the Historical Jesus*, p. 396.

19. As Günther Bornkam reflected: 'It became alarmingly and terrifyingly evident how inevitably

each author brought the spirit of his own age into his presentation of the figure of Jesus.' Günther Bornkam, *Jesus of Nazareth*, Hodder & Stoughton, 1960, p. 13.

20. Schweitzer, *The Quest of the Historical Jesus*, p. 397.

21. Bornkam, *Jesus of Nazareth*, 1960, p. 13.

2 The Quest for the Historical Jesus in the Twentieth Century and Beyond

1. Rudolf Bultmann, *Theology of the New Testament*, 2 volumes, Scribner, 1951–55.

2. The German original appeared in 1956. The English edition appeared a few years later. Günther Bornkam, *Jesus of Nazareth*, Hodder & Stoughton, 1960, p. 9.

3. Ernst Käsemann, *Essays on New Testament Themes*, SCM, 1964, pp. 15–47.

4. Bornkam, *Jesus of Nazareth*; Norman Perrin, *Rediscovering the Teaching of Jesus*, SCM, 1967.

5. See for example 1 Corinthians 3:11 and Matthew 7:25.

6. Geza Vermes, *The Authentic Gospel of Jesus*, Penguin, 2003, p. 374.

7. R. Funk and R. W. Hoover (eds.), *The Five Gospels: The Search for the Authentic Words of Jesus*, Macmillan, 1993.

8. See his criticisms in James Dunn, *Jesus Remembered*, Eerdmans, 2003, pp. 58–65 (this particular quotation is on p. 64).

9. Indicative of this move toward understanding Jesus in his Jewish context is the following volume containing essays by contemporary Jewish and non-Jewish scholars: James H. Charlesworth (ed.), *Jesus' Jewishness: Exploring the Place of Jesus within Early Judaism*, Crossroad Publishing, 1991. It is also striking that a major chapter on Jesus appears in *The Cambridge History of Judaism*, vol. III, edited by William Horbury et al.: *The Early Roman Period*, Cambridge University Press, 2001.

10. Many young and old scholars would admit to being keen admirers of Martin Hengel. Few scholars find themselves the subject of a full celebratory article in a peer-reviewed journal. However, see Roland Deines, 'Martin Hengel: A Life in Service of Christology', *Tyndale Bulletin* 58/1, 2007, pp. 26–42.

11. Martin Hengel, *The Zealots*, T. & T. Clark, 1989.

12. Martin Hengel, *Judaism and Hellenism: Studies in Their Encounter in Palestine During the Early Hellenistic Period*, Fortress Press, 1975.

13. The new edition of the 1968 classic is Martin Hengel, *The Charismatic Leader and His Followers*, Wipf & Stock, 2005.

14. The new edition of this 1976 classic is Martin Hengel, *The Son of God: The Origin of Christology and the History of Jewish Hellenistic Religion*, Wipf & Stock, 2007.

15. E. P. Sanders, *Judaism: Practice and Belief, 63 BCE–66 CE*, SCM Press, 1992.

16. E. P. Sanders, *Jesus and Judaism*, Fortress Press, 1985.

17. The quotation comes from Tom Wright's 2nd revised edition of Stephen Neill, *The Interpretation of the New Testament, 1861–1986*, Oxford University Press (1964), 1988, p. 379.

18. N. T. Wright, *The New Testament and the People of God*, Fortress Press, 1992.

19. N. T. Wright, *Jesus and the Victory of God*, Fortress Press, 1996.

20. Dunn, *Jesus Remembered*, p. 87.

3 A Brief History Lesson

1. Martin Hengel, *Acts and the History of Earliest Christianity*, Wipf & Stock, 2003, p. 130.

2. The Greek text, translation and comment can be found in *New Documents Illustrating Early Christianity*, vol. IX, edited by S. R. Llewelyn, Eerdmans, 2002, pp. 42–44.

3. N. Krieger, 'Fiktive Orte der Johannestaufe', *Zeitschrift für die Neutestamentliche Wissenschaft und die Kunde der Älteren Kirche* 45, 1954, pp. 121–23; John Marsh, *The Gospel of Saint John*, Penguin Books, 1968, pp. 245–6. It may seem odd that Marsh would propose a symbolic interpretation of John 5:2 when archaeological investigations had uncovered the five colonnade pool of Bethesda by 1962. Perhaps it is because the official reports, prepared by archaeologists J.-M. Rousée and R. de Vaux, were published in French: J.-M. Rousée, 'Chroniques Archéologiques', *Revue Biblique* 69, 1962, pp. 107–109. Nevertheless, two years before Marsh's commentary appeared, a full English account of the Bethesda discovery was offered by the great New Testament historian Joachim Jeremias: *The Rediscovery of Bethesda, John 5:2, New Testament Archaeology Monographs* 1, Southern Baptist Theological Seminary, 1966.

4. For the details of the Bethesda discoveries see Urban C. von Wahlde, 'Archaeology and John's Gospel', in James H. Charlesworth (ed.), *Jesus and Archaeology*, Eerdmans, 2006, pp. 560–66.

5. Von Wahlde, 'Archaeology and John's Gospel', p. 566.

6. Graham Stanton, *The Gospels and Jesus*, 2nd edition, Oxford University Press, 2003, p. 144.

7. Chris Gaffney, 'The Origins of Christianity: From Jewish Revolution to a State Religion', *Australian Rationalist* 71, 2005, p. 21.

8. For instance, the main source of our knowledge of Emperor Tiberius (died AD 37) is Tacitus' Annals, written more than seventy years later.

9. John Dickson, 'Gaffney's Gaffs on the Historical Jesus', *Australian Rationalist* 73, 2006, pp. 51–52.

10. See Gerd Theissen and Annette Merz, *The Historical Jesus: A Comprehensive Guide*, Fortress Press, 1998, p. 93.

11. Michel Onfray, *The Atheist Manifesto*, Arcade Publishing, 2005, p. 117.

12. Christopher Tuckett, 'Sources and Methods', in *The Cambridge Companion to Jesus*, ed. Marcus Bockmuehl, Cambridge University Press, 2001, p. 124.

13. E. P. Sanders, *The Historical Figure of Jesus*, Penguin Books, 1993, p.11. Although not reflected in this quotation, Sanders (along with most experts in the field) regards it as equally certain that Jesus performed deeds which friend and foe alike believed to be miraculous (see Chapter 10 of his book). It is beyond the task of the historian to judge whether such a belief in miracles is valid; history can only uncover the fact that Jesus' actions were interpreted as miraculous by those around him.

4 The Gnostic Gospels

1. Dan Brown, *The Da Vinci Code*, Bantam Press, 2003, pp. 231–34.

2. See Martin Hengel, *The Four Gospels and the One Gospel of Jesus Christ*, Trinity Press, 2000.

3. The most authoritative volume on the question of the development of the canon remains the one by Professor Bruce M. Metzger of Princeton University, *The Canon of the New Testament: Its Origin, Development and Significance*, Oxford University Press, 1997.

4. See David Brakke, 'The Gnostics and Their Opponents', in *The Cambridge History of Christianity*, vol. I, edited by Margaret M. Mitchell and Frances M. Young: Origins to Constantine, Cambridge University Press, 2006, pp. 245–60.

5. Kurt Rudolph, 'Gnosticism', in *The Anchor Bible Dictionary*, vol. II, Doubleday, 1992, pp. 1033–44.

6. For further details see N. T. Wright's *Judas and the Gospel of Jesus*, SPCK, 2006.

7. *Gospel of Judas* 1. The translation is that of Rodolphe Kasser, Marvin Meyer and Gregor Wurst for the National Geographic Society, 2006.

8. A date of AD 160 would be the earliest possible for the composition of the Gospel of Philip, since it displays a developed version of the views of the Gnostic leader Valentinus, who was in Rome between 138 and 158. See further Wilhelm Schneemelcher (ed.), *New Testament Apocrypha, vol. I: Gospels and Related Writings*, James Clarke & Co., 1991, pp. 179–87.

9. The translation is that of Hans-Martin Schenke in Schneemelcher (ed.), *New Testament Apocrypha*, vol. 1, p. 194.

10. Brown, *The Da Vinci Code*, p. 244. A more serious attempt to argue that Jesus was married is William E. Phipps, *Was Jesus Married? The Distortion of Sexuality in the Christian Tradition*, Harper & Row, 1970. As the subtitle makes clear, Phipps has a strong anti-Christian, or rather anti-Roman Catholic, agenda. His handling of the evidence is not unaffected by this apologetic aim. See the gentlemanly demolition of his argument by John P. Meier, *A Marginal Jew*, vol. I, Doubleday, 1991, pp. 332–45, 363–65.

11. Peter Nagel, 'Gnosis, Gnosticism', *The Encyclopedia of Christianity*, vol. II, Eerdmans and Brill, 2001, p. 419.

12. Gospel of Thomas 1. The translation is that of Beate Blatz in Schneemelcher (ed.), *New Testament Apocrypha*, vol. 1, p. 117.

13. Schneemelcher (ed.), *New Testament Apocrypha*, vol. I, p. 113.

14. Graham Stanton, *The Gospels and Jesus*, 2nd edition, Oxford University Press, 2003, p.129

15. The Jesus Seminar mentioned in Chapter 1 elevates the Gospel of Thomas to one the most important sources, as does the brilliant John Dominic Crossan. See, for example, R. Funk and R. W. Hoover (eds.), *The Five Gospels: The Search for the Authentic Words of Jesus*, Macmillan, 1993; John Dominic Crossan, *The Historical Jesus*, HarperSanFrancisco, 1991. Such views fail to convince many in scholarship.

16. Meier, *A Marginal Jew*, pp. 140–41.

Did Jesus marry?

1. Brown, The Da Vinci Code, p. 245.

2. Jeremiah 16:1–4 reads: 'Then the word of the Lord came to me: "You must not marry and have sons or daughters in this place." For this is what the Lord says about the sons and daughters born in this land

and about the women who are their mothers and the men who are their fathers: "They will die of deadly diseases. They will not be mourned or buried but will be like dung lying on the ground. They will perish by sword and famine, and their dead bodies will become food for the birds and the wild animals.'"

3. Many, though not all, of the Essene Jews were celibate. See Otto Betz, 'The Essenes', in William Horbury et al. (eds.), *The Cambridge History of Judaism, vol. III: The Early Roman Period*, Cambridge University Press, 2001, pp. 458–59. Josephus mentions the Essenes' practice of celibacy, but makes it clear that they do not condemn wedlock in principle (Josephus, Jewish War 2.121).

4. The Alexandrian Jewish intellectual Philo (10 BC–AD 50) wrote an entire book on the ascetic life of the Therapeutae, On the Contemplative Life. See Meier, *A Marginal Jew*, vol. I, Doubleday, 1991, pp. 337–38.

5. Jesus' teaching on marriage can be found in Mark 10:2–12 (repeated in Matthew 19:3–9) and Matthew 5:31–32. The evidence for the marriages of Jesus' apostles and brothers (some of them, anyway) can be found in Mark 1:30 and 1 Corinthians 9:5.

Some inauthentic sayings from the Gospel of Thomas

1. See Graham Stanton, *The Gospels and Jesus*. 2nd edition, Oxford University Press, 2003, pp.125–26

5 Non-Christian References to Jesus from the Second Century

1. Some important Hebrew manuscripts of the Talmud are housed in the Bayerische Staatsbibliothek, the Royal Library of Munich, Ludwigstrasse, Munich, Germany, and in Cambridge University Library, West Road, Cambridge, UK.

2. So Robert Van Voorst, *Jesus Outside the New Testament: An Introduction to the Ancient Evidence*, Eerdmans, 2000, p. 117. Theissen places it in the 'early second century': Theissen and Merz, *The Historical Jesus*, p. 75.

3. This translation appears in Theissen and Merz, *The Historical Jesus*, p. 75.

4. It is sometimes thought that the second-century Jewish philosopher Trypho disputed the existence of Jesus when debating with the Christian philosopher Justin. This is a misreading of the text. When Trypho is reported as saying that Christians 'invented a Christ' (Justin, *Dialogue with Trypho 8*), he does not mean that the man Jesus never lived;

only, as the context makes clear, that ascribing to this man the status of the Christ or Messiah is an invention. In other places, Trypho clearly assumes the existence of Jesus: 'But prove to us that Jesus Christ is the one about whom these prophecies were spoken ...' (*Dialogue with Trypho 36*). Again, the argument is over whether Old Testament prophecies about the Messiah are fulfilled in Jesus.

5. Craig A. Evans (ed.), *Encyclopedia of the Historical Jesus*, Routledge, 2007, p. 605.

6. Justin Martyr, *Dialogue with Trypho 69*.

7. The surviving Latin manuscripts of Tacitus' Annals are stored in the Laurentian Library (Piazza del Duomo, Florence, Italy).

8. Rumours soon circulated among the upper classes of Rome that Nero himself had started the fire because he wanted to refurbish parts of the city. Whether or not he was behind it, on the night of the fire Nero was 30 miles away at his villa in Antium.

9. The translation is that of John Jackson in *Tacitus: Annals 13–16*, Loeb Classical Library, vol. 322, Harvard University Press, 1999, p. 283.

10. The relevant manuscript of Pliny's Letters is stored in the Morgan Library, East 36th Street, New York. The translation is that of Betty Radice in *Pliny: Letters and Panegyricus*, Books 8–10, Loeb Classical Library, vol. 59, Harvard University Press, 1962, p. 289.

11. Theissen and Merz, *The Historical Jesus*, p. 81.

How to read the non-Christian texts about Jesus

1. Michel Onfray, *The Atheist Manifesto*, Arcade Publishing, 2005, p. 117.

2. Gerd Theissen and Annette Merz, *The Historical Jesus: A Comprehensive Guide*, Fortress Press, 1998, p. 63.

6 Non-Christian References to Jesus from the First Century

1. Important manuscripts of Josephus' *Antiquities* are stored in the Biblioteca Ambrosiana (the Ambrosian Library), Piazza Pio XI, Milan, Italy, and in the Vatican Library, via Santa Anna's Gate, Vatican City, Italy.

2. The translation is that of Louis H. Feldman in *Sidonius: Letters*, Books 3–9, Loeb Classical Library, vol. 456, Harvard University Press, 1996, pp. 107–109.

3. Gerd Theissen and Annette Merz, *The Historical Jesus: A Comprehensive Guide*, Fortress Press, 1998, p. 65.

4. The brothers of Jesus are named in Mark 6:3. Their travels as missionaries are referred to in 1 Corinthians 9:5. James's leadership of the Jerusalem church is mentioned in Acts 15:13; 21:18 and in Galatians 1:19; 2:9.

5. Graham Stanton, *The Gospels and Jesus*, 2nd edition, Oxford University Press, 2003, p. 148.

6. Jewish Antiquities 18.63–64. The translation is that of Louis H. Feldman in *Josephus, vol. XII: Jewish Antiquities*, Books 18–19, Loeb Classical Library, vol. 433, Harvard University Press, 1996, pp. 49–51.

7. For example, F. C. Burkitt, 'Josephus and Christ', *Theologisch Tijdschrift* 47, 1913, pp. 135–44; F. Dornseiff, 'Zum Testimonium Flavium', *Zeitschrift für die neutestamentliche Wissenschaft* 46, 1955, pp. 245–50.

8. For example, S. Zeitlin, 'The Christ Passage in Josephus', *Jewish Quarterly Review* 18, 1927–8), pp. 231–55.

9. 'We do not know who the Christian interpolator(s) were, or whether indeed the interpolations are anything more than random marginal notes that entered the text at different times.' John P. Meier, *A Marginal Jew*, vol. I, Doubleday, 1991, p. 79.

10. The arguments about the phraseology of this passage are discussed in great detail in Meier, *A Marginal Jew*, vol. I, pp. 59–88.

11. Stanton, *The Gospels and Jesus*, 2nd edition, p. 150. See also S. G. F. Brandon, 'The Testimonium Flavium', *History Today* 19 (1969), p. 438; Louis H. Feldman, 'The Testimonium Flavium: The State of the Question', in R. F. Berkey and S. A. Edwards (eds.), *Christological Perspectives* (New York: Pilgrim, 1982), pp. 179–99, pp. 288–93; Geza Vermes, 'The Jesus Notice of Josephus Re-examined', *Journal of Jewish Studies* 38, 1987, pp. 1–10; Meier, *A Marginal Jew*, vol. I, pp. 56–69; Theissen and Merz, *The Historical Jesus*, pp. 65–74; Robert Van Voorst, *Jesus Outside the New Testament: An Introduction to the Ancient Evidence*, Eerdmans, 2000, pp. 84–104; Christopher Tuckett, 'Sources and Methods', in *The Cambridge Companion to Jesus*, ed. Marcus Bockmuehl, Cambridge University Press, 2001, pp. 123–4; James Dunn, *Jesus Remembered*, Eerdmans, 2003, p. 141.

12. Meier, *A Marginal Jew*, vol. I, p. 68.

13. The date is disputed, but Theissen and Merz suggest: 'Probably, it was composed soon after 73 CE': *The Historical Jesus*, p. 77. A similar date is suggested by Craig A. Evans, *Noncanonical Writings and New Testament Interpretation*, Hendrickson, 1992, p. 171. Robert Van Voorst places

it in the second century, but admits that 'most date it to the first century, shortly after the Roman conquest of Commagene in 73 to which the author seems to refer': *Jesus Outside the New Testament*, p. 56.

14. The modern description of someone as 'stoic' comes from the original Stoics' insistence that true happiness is found in conquering one's passions with intellectual insight – emotion controlled by mind.

15. That is, the residents of the Island of Samos off the west coast of modern Turkey.

16. This translation is found in Theissen and Merz, *The Historical Jesus*, p. 77. The original Syriac and translation are found in W. Cureton, *Spicilegium Syriacum*, London: Francis and John Rivington, 1855, pp. 43–48 (Syriac), 70–76 (English).

17. The most recent scholarly article on the letter suggests that 'it is more than reasonable to suppose that the "wise king" here is meant to be a reference to Jesus. This has been the general consensus of scholars working on the letter since Cureton [in 1855]': Catherine M. Chin, 'Rhetorical Practice in the Chreia Elaboration of Mara bar Serapion', *Hugoye: Journal of Syriac Studies* 9/2, 2006, p. 21.

18. Here I am disagreeing with Theissen and Merz, *The Historical Jesus*, pp. 78–79), who make too much of the fact that 'king' is a theme of Christian reflection about Jesus. In fact, the word 'king' is rarely applied to Jesus as a title. And, more importantly, Mara repeats the description 'wise king' as though it were his stock epithet for Jesus. So far as we can tell, that does not come from Christians.

19. There is evidence that Thallos was a Samaritan (i.e., a resident of Samaria in the middle of ancient Palestine) with strong connections also with Rome. On this see Emil Schurer, revised and edited by Geza Vermes, Fergus Millar and Martin Goodman, *The History of the Jewish People in the Age of Jesus Christ*, vol. III, pt.1, T. &T. Clark, 1987, pp. 543–5. For a detailed discussion of the Thallos reference to Jesus see Van Voorst, *Jesus Outside the New Testament*, pp. 20–23.

20. The translation is my own. The relevant text in Greek is printed in F. Jacoby, *Die Fragmente der griechischen Historiker*, vol. II, Brill, 1962, p. 1157.

21. Assessing a report of a report is a normal part of historical investigation. Indeed, entire academic volumes today are dedicated to publishing such fragmentary citations of ancient authors, such as the one in which the Thallos citation appears (see note 24).

22. Theissen and Merz, *The Historical Jesus*, p. 85; so also Van Voorst, *Jesus Outside the New Testament*, p. 21.

23. The literacy levels of ancient Mediterranean societies in this period are discussed in William V. Harris, *Ancient Literacy*, Harvard University Press, 1989, pp. 175–284.

24. Michel Onfray, *The Atheist Manifesto*, Arcade Publishing, 2005, pp. 115–16.

25. Tuckett, 'Sources and Methods', p. 124.

26. Theissen and Merz, *The Historical Jesus*, pp. 93–94.

27. Charlesworth, *The Historical Jesus*, p. 35.

What we learn from Josephus

1. The translation is that of H. St. J. Thackeray in Josephus, vol. II: *The Jewish War*, Books 1–2, Loeb Classical Library, vol. 203, Harvard University Press, 1989, pp. 369, 385–87.

An Arabic Version of Josephus

1. Shlomo Pines, *An Arabic Version of the Testimonium Flavianum and its Implications*, Israel Academy of Sciences and Humanities, 1971, p. 69.

2 Some have retorted that the hesitation in Agapius' version was added by the bishop himself to avoid controversy with Muslims in his Islamic context. See E. Bammel, 'A New Variant Form of the Testimonium Flavianum', *Judaica*, WUNT 37, Mohr Siebeck, 1987, pp. 190–93. This makes no sense at all, since Muslims readily affirm Jesus as 'Christ'; it is his divinity they reject. Agapius would have gained nothing by softening 'he was the Christ' to 'he was perhaps the Messiah'.

3. James H. Charlesworth, *The Historical Jesus: An Essential Guide*, Abingdon Press, 2008, p. 35.

4. John P. Meier makes the case that Josephus' statements about Jesus are unlikely to have come from any Christian source (whether written or oral): *A Marginal Jew*, vol. I, p. 67.

When scholarly opinion isn't relevant

1. These words are not my verbatim recollection after more than two decades. I recently found them quoted by James Dunn, Professor of Divinity at the University of Durham, in his response to the documentary in *The Evidence for Jesus: The Impact of Scholarship on Our Understanding of How Christianity Began*, SCM Press, 1985, p. 1.

2. Meier, *A Marginal Jew*, vol. I, p. 87.

7   The New Testament Records about Jesus

1. Richard Dawkins, *The God Delusion*, Bantam Press, 2006, p. 97.

2. Statements similar to Dawkins's are found in Michel Onfray, *The Atheist Manifesto*, pp. 125–6, and Christopher Hitchens, *God is Not Great: How Religion Poisons Everything*, Twelve, 2007, pp. 112–15.

3. Daniel Reisberg and Friderike Heuer, 'Memory for Emotional Events', in Daniel Reisberg and Paula Hertel (eds.), *Memory and Emotion*, Oxford University Press, 2004, p. 35. Reisberg is Professor of Psychology at Reed College in Portland, Oregon, and Heuer is a former Professor of Psychology at Lewis and Clark College in Portland, Oregon.

4. Bauckham, *Jesus and the Eyewitnesses*, p. 346. The whole of chapter 13 (pp. 319–57) is devoted to a review of the psychological literature and its relevance to studying the historical Jesus.

5. The precise date of each of Paul's letters is not known, but it is certain that he wrote between AD 50 and 64. On the chronology of Paul see Rainer Riesner, *Paul's Early Period: Chronology, Mission Strategy, Theology*, Eerdmans, 1998. The historical source for the martyrdom of Paul (by beheading) is Eusebius, Ecclesiastical History 2.25.5–6. There is no reason to doubt the account.

6. Dawkins, *The God Delusion*, p. 93.

7. The full interview with Professor Stuhlmacher can be viewed in episode 2 of *The Christ Files DVD*, Blue Bottle Books, 2008.

8. An important book on the question of Paul and Jesus is David Wenham, *Paul: Follower of Jesus or Founder of Christianity?*, Eerdmans, 1995.

9. See further Ben F. Meyer, *The Aims of Jesus*, SCM, 1979, pp. 74–75, 275–76.

10. Chris Gaffney, 'The Origins of Christianity: From Jewish Revolution to a State Religion', *Australian Rationalist* 71, 2005, pp. 21–27.

11. Donald Harman Akenson, *Saint Saul: A Skeleton Key to the Historical Jesus*, Oxford University Press, 2000, p. 173. I disagree with parts of Akenson's argument. For instance, he suggests that the reason Paul fails to narrate the stories and sayings of Jesus in his letters is that, for the apostle, only the post-earthly Christ, not the historical Jesus, was relevant to the ongoing complexities of his non-Jewish churches. This overlooks the central place of the cross in Paul's thinking about ethics and sociology – surely, the crucifixion is part of the historical Jesus. There is not nearly as much reliance in Paul's letters on the post-earthly exalted vision of Christ

as Akenson seems to think. When Paul responds to crises in his churches, he tends to rely neither on the earthly story of Jesus nor on the exalted figure of Christ, but on various religious principles drawn from Jewish Scripture, logic, and especially the fact of the Messiah's death on our behalf. Moreover, one only needs a small taste of Christian ministry, of which letter-writing is a significant part, to realize that many issues faced by believers cannot be settled with a quotation from Jesus' life. But this does not for a moment mean that the Jesus story is irrelevant to the thinking of the pastor – likewise Paul. The reason Paul does not narrate stories and sayings of Jesus in his letters is simple: the Jesus story was the founding message of Paul – as is clear from the passing references he makes to that story – whereas the letters are designed to answer various ethical, social and theological questions raised in his communities. Akenson calls this explanation 'facile and familiar' (p. 173). 'Familiar' it is – many scholars accept it – but he does not explain why it is 'facile', other than that it contradicts his own theory.

12. Paula Fredriksen, *Jesus of Nazareth: King of the Jews*, Vintage Books, 2000, p. 77. Her methodology is laid out on pp. 74–78.

13. This is widely recognized and any serious commentary on 1 Corinthians will bear out the point. For further information on how this Jewish oral tradition functioned, see Birger Gerhardsson, *The Reliability of the Gospel Tradition*, Hendrickson, 2001.

14. Given that Paul was preaching Jesus as the Christ and Son of God for three years before he arrived in Jerusalem, 'Damascus is the preferred option', writes New Testament historian Paul Barnett, *The Birth of Christianity: The First Twenty Years*, Eerdmans, 2005, p. 87.

15. Paul refers to this meeting with Peter and James in Galatians 1:18–20.

16. James D. G. Dunn, *Jesus Remembered*, Eerdmans, 2003, p. 855.

17. For example, G. Lüdemann, *What Really Happened to Jesus: A Historical Approach to the Resurrection*, Westminster John Knox Press, 1995, pp. 14–15; R. Funk, *The Acts of Jesus: The Search for the Authentic Deeds of Jesus*, Harper, 1998, p. 466.

18. *P46* is a copy of Paul's letters dated to about AD 200 – though, as the curator of the collection pointed out to me, some scholars have begun to argue for an even earlier date.

19. Dunn, *Jesus Remembered*. Other important works include Gerhardsson, *The Reliability of the Gospel Tradition*; and Bauckham, *Jesus and the Eyewitnesses*. I have offered a popular treatment

of the subject in *The Christ Files: How Historians Know What They Know about Jesus*, Blue Bottle Books, 2005, pp. 57–70.

20. For further details on how the word 'gospel' was used in the ancient world see John P. Dickson, 'Gospel as News: euaggel- from Aristophanes to the Apostle Paul', in *New Testament Studies* 51, 2005, pp. 221–30.

21. Isaiah, of course, wrote in Hebrew, but in the Greek version of the Old Testament, often quoted in the New Testament, the word euangelizesthai ('to tell a gospel') is used.

22. Chapter 5 of my doctoral thesis focused on the importance of Isaiah's gospel herald for Jesus' self-understanding: John P. Dickson, *Mission-Commitment in Ancient Judaism and in the Pauline Communities*, WUNT II 159, Mohr Siebeck, 2003, pp. 153–77. See also the excellent analysis of the importance of Isaiah 61 for Jesus in W. D. Davies and Dale C. Allison, *The Gospel According to Saint Matthew*, vol. I, T, & T, Clark, 1988, pp, 436–41.

23. There used to be debate among scholars about exactly when these titles ('The Gospel according to Matthew', 'The Gospel according to Mark', etc.) were added to the works. Some proposed the late second century. But Martin Hengel of the University of Tübingen in Germany has now established that these titles, if not original to the works, were probably added as soon as the Gospels began to be copied. It is telling that all our many ancient manuscripts of these Gospels contain the Greek words euangelion kata ... ('Gospel according to ...'). See Martin Hengel, *The Four Gospels and the One Gospel of Jesus Christ*, Trinity Press, 2000, pp. 50–56.

24. John Shelby Spong, *Jesus for the Non-Religious*, HarperCollins, 2007, p. 157.

25. Graham Stanton, *Jesus of Nazareth in New Testament Preaching*, Cambridge University Press, 1974 (Chapter 5 discusses ancient biography).

26. Richard Burridge, *What are the Gospels? A Comparison with Graeco-Roman Biography*, Cambridge University Press, 1992.

27. The full interview with Professor Bauckham can be viewed in episode 2 of *The Christ Files DVD*.

28. David Flusser, 'Jesus, His Ancestry and the Commandment to Love', in James H. Charlesworth (ed.), *Jesus' Jewishness*, Crossroad, 1991, p. 154 (italics original). Professor Flusser died on 15 September 2000, on his eighty-third birthday.

Can bias be useful?

1. Lawrence L. Langer, *Holocaust Testimonies: The Ruins of Memory*, Yale University Press, 1991.

The *bios* genre

1. Agricola ordered his fleet to circumnavigate Britain and thus confirmed that it was an island.

2. When asked what sort of funeral he would like, Demonax replied, 'Don't go to any trouble.' He was quite happy to be left to the birds and dogs. 'It's not in the least disgusting if even when I'm dead I can be of use to living creatures,' he said (*Lucian Demonax* 67). As it turned out, Athens threw a splendid public funeral for him.

3. Loveday Alexander, 'What is a Gospel?', in Stephen C. Barton (ed.), *The Cambridge Companion to the Gospels*, Cambridge University Press, 2006, pp. 13–33.

8   Sources in the Gospels

1. Richard Burridge, *What are the Gospels? A Comparison with Graeco-Roman Biography*, Cambridge University Press, 1992, p. 120.

2. Eusebius, *Ecclesiastical History* 3.39.15. The translation is that of Kirsopp Lake in *Eusebius: Ecclesiastical History*, Books I–V, Loeb Classical Library, vol.153, Harvard University Press, 1998, p. 297.

3. Martin Hengel, *The Four Gospels and the One Gospel of Jesus Christ*, Trinity Press, 2000, pp. 65–68.

4. It is clear from other evidence that Mark was less popular than the other three Gospels.

5. The influence of the teaching of Peter in the first twenty years of Christianity is explored in Paul Barnett, *The Birth of Christianity: The First Twenty Years*, Eerdmans, 2005, pp. 86–94.

6. A balanced account of these Gospel sources is offered by Robert Van Voorst, *Jesus Outside the New Testament: An Introduction to the Ancient Evidence*, Eerdmans, 2000.

7. The full interview with Christopher Tuckett may be viewed in episode 3 of *The Christ Files DVD*, Blue Bottle Books, 2008. His major book on the subject is *Q and the History of Early Christianity*, T. & T. Clark, 1996.

8. For example, Darrell L. Bock, Luke 1:1 – 9:50, *Baker Exegetical Commentary on the New Testament*, Baker, 1994, pp. 16–18.

9. Martin Hengel, *Acts and the History of Earliest Christianity*, Wipf and Stock, 2003, p. 66. See also the earlier judgment of the distinguished Lukan scholar Joseph A. Fitzmyer, The Gospel According to Luke, vol. I, *The Anchor Bible*, vol. 28a, Doubleday, 1970, pp. 47–51.

10. I. Howard Marshall, *The Gospel of Luke*, New International Greek Testament Commentary, Eerdmans, 1978, p. 31.

11. A comprehensive study of this question is Kim Paffenroth, The Story of Jesus according to L, *Journal for the Study of the New Testament Supplement Series 147*, Sheffield Academic Press, 1997.

12. See the detailed discussion in W. D. Davies and Dale C. Allison, *The Gospel According to Saint Matthew*, vol. I, T. & T. Clark, 1988, pp. 127–38.

13. For example, Donald A. Hagner, Matthew 1–13, *Word Biblical Commentary* 33a, Thomas Nelson, 1993, pp. xliii–lxxi.

14. Davies and Allison, *The Gospel According to Saint Matthew*, vol. I, p. 125.

15. The major works exploring the Signs Source are Robert T. Fortna, *The Gospel of Signs*, Cambridge University Press, 1970; and Urban C. von Wahlde, *The Earliest Version of John's Gospel*, Glazier, 1989.

An eyewitness source

1. Richard Bauckham, *Jesus and the Eyewitnesses*, Eerdmans, 2006, p. 204. So too Hengel, *The Four Gospels and the One Gospel of Jesus Christ*, p. 82.

2. Bauckham, *Jesus and the Eyewitnesses*, p. 204.

9   Testing the Gospel Story

1. The so-called Jesus Seminar in the USA still applies the criterion of dissimilarity. As I said in Chapter 1, the Seminar represents a strange throwback to the aspirations and methods of a previous generation of scholars.

2. The teaching is, however, repeated in the New Testament letter of James, at 5:12.

3. Ben F. Meyer, *The Aims of Jesus*, SCM, 1979, p. 87.

4. John Shelby Spong, *Jesus for the Non-Religious*, HarperCollins, 2007, p. 38.

5. Meyer, *The Aims of Jesus*, pp. 153–4; James H. Charlesworth, *Jesus Within Judaism: New Light from Exciting Archaeological Discoveries*, 1988, pp. 136–8; E. P. Sanders, *The Historical Figure of Jesus*, Penguin Books, 1993, pp. 118–22; John P. Meier, *A Marginal Jew*, vol. II, Doubleday, 1994,

pp. 128–47; N. T. Wright, *Jesus and the Victory of God*, Fortress Press, 1996, pp. 299–300; Paula Fredriksen, *Jesus of Nazareth: King of the Jews*, Vintage Books, 1997, pp. 89–98; Gerd Theissen and Annette Merz, *The Historical Jesus: A Comprehensive Guide*, Fortress Press, 1998, pp. 216–17; Dale C. Allison, *Jesus of Nazareth: Millenarian Prophet*, Fortress Press, 1998, p. 101; Bruce Chilton, 'Friends and Enemies', in Marcus Bockmuehl (ed.), *The Cambridge Companion to Jesus*, Cambridge University Press, 2001, p. 81; James Dunn, *Jesus Remembered*, Eerdmans, 2003, pp. 507–11; Graham Stanton, *The Gospels and Jesus*, 2nd edition, Oxford University Press, 2003, p. 201; Sean Freyne, *Jesus, a Jewish Galilean: A New Reading of the Jesus-Story*, T. & T. Clark, 2005, p. 119; Martin Hengel, *The Charismatic Leader and His Followers*, Wipf & Stock, 2005, pp. 60, 68; Richard Bauckham, *Jesus and the Eyewitnesses*, Eerdmans, 2006, pp. 93–113.

6. Some of the greatest preachers and prophets of ancient Israel physically embodied their message in vivid ways (Hosea 1:2–9; Jeremiah 16:2–4; Ezekiel 4:1–13). In the period of Jesus himself, John the Baptist continued this prophetic tradition, demanding that all Israelites enter the Jordan river – where centuries earlier they had begun their entry into the Promised Land – as a symbol of a new beginning. And in AD 57 a man known as Agabus warned the apostle Paul of impending imprisonment, not simply by telling him but, in true prophetic style, by taking Paul's belt and tying himself up in it (Acts 21:10–11). In this context Jesus' selection of twelve men as a symbol of Israel's twelve tribes is precisely the sort of thing we should expect from someone with a keen sense of his prophetic call to Israel.

7. The Twelve are attested in Mark (3:14; 4:10; 6:7; 9:35; 10:32; 11:11; 14:10), in Q (Matthew 19:28; Luke 22:29–30), in John (6:70; 20:24), in Paul (1 Corinthians 15:5) and in L (Luke 6:13–16; Acts 1:13). It may be thought that Luke is dependent on Mark for his list of the Twelve in Luke 6:13–16. However, there are good grounds for thinking that Luke had a list of the Twelve different from Mark's (containing 'Judas son of James' instead of 'Thaddaeus'). When we note that this name is also attested in John 14:22, 'the most natural explanation is that Luke found this name in a list he inherited from his L tradition': Meier, *A Marginal Jew*, vol. II, p. 133.

8. Bishop Spong is quite wide of the mark when he suggests that it was only in the mid-50s that 'Paul introduces the concept of the "twelve" into the Christian story': Spong, *Jesus for the Non-Religious*, p. 38.

9. Theissen and Merz, *The Historical Jesus*, p. 94.

10. Dunn, *Jesus Remembered*, pp. 832–3.

11. *Jewish Antiquities* 4.219.

12. *Mishnah Shabuot* 4.1

13. Stanton, *The Gospels and Jesus*, pp. 289–90.

14. For scholarly accounts of these issues see Richard Bauckham, *Gospel Women: Studies in the Named Women in the Gospels*, Eerdmans, 2002, pp. 268–77; Dunn, *Jesus Remembered*, pp. 832–33; Stanton, *The Gospels and Jesus*, 2nd edition, pp. 289–320; N. T. Wright, *The Resurrection of the Son of God*, SPCK, 2003, pp. 607–8; Theissen and Merz, *The Historical Jesus*, pp. 495–9.

Were there really twelve apostles?

1. Charlesworth, *Jesus Within Judaism*, p. 137.

2. Meyer, *The Aims of Jesus*, p. 154.

10 Assessing Historical Plausibility

1. For a brief introduction to the philosophy of history and, in particular, the distinction between historical 'data' and 'facts', see Ben F. Meyer, *The Aims of Jesus*, SCM, 1979, pp. 87–92.

2. John P. Meier, *A Marginal Jew: Rethinking the Historical Jesus*, vol. I, Doubleday, 1991, p. 176.

3. Meier, *A Marginal Jew*, p. 176.

4. Charlesworth, *The Historical Jesus*, p. 25.

5. Charlesworth, *The Historical Jesus*, p. 25.

6. On the date, provenance and themes of the text see R. B. Wright, 'Psalms of Solomon', in James H. Charlesworth (ed.), The Old Testament Pseudepigrapha, vol. II, Doubleday, 1985, pp. 639–70. The translation used is that of Wright.

7. *Damascus Document* 11.13–17.

8. James H. Charlesworth, 'The Dead Sea Scrolls and the Historical Jesus', in James H. Charlesworth (ed.), *Jesus and the Dead Sea Scrolls*, Doubleday, 1992, p. 34.

9. Meier, *A Marginal Jew*, vol. I, p. 265. Important Aramaic studies include Matthew Black, *An Aramaic Approach to the Gospels and Acts*, Clarendon Press, 1946; and Joseph A. Fitzmyer, *The Semitic Background of the New Testament*, combined edition of *Essays on the Semitic Background of the New Testament and A Wandering Aramean: Collected Aramaic Essays*, Eerdmans and Dove, 1997.

10. Luke (11:4) changes the word to 'sins', presumably to make this clearer.

11. Meier, *A Marginal Jew*, vol. II, p. 265.

12. See Craig A. Evans, Mark 8:27 – 16:20, *Word Biblical Commentary*, vol. 34b, Thomas Nelson, 2001, pp. 412–13. It is striking to note that the same phenomenon can be found in two of the apostle Paul's letters. Writing in Greek to the Christians of Galatia (northern Turkey), he says: 'Because you are his sons, God sent the Spirit of his Son into our hearts, the Spirit who calls out, "Abba, Father",' (Galatians 4:6). And to the Romans he writes similarly: 'The Spirit you received does not make you slaves, so that you live in fear again; rather, the Spirit you received brought about your adoption to sonship. And by him we cry, "Abba, Father",' (Romans 8:15).

13. The Latin-speaking Romans had ruled the world for a century or more by the time of Jesus, but there was nothing they could do to erase the universal currency of the Greek language that had resulted from the success of the literary and philosophical traditions of Greece and the enormous military expansion of Alexander the Great. If you wanted to get on in the Roman empire, you spoke Greek.

14. Martin Hengel, *Judaism and Hellenism: Studies in Their Encounter in Palestine During the Early Hellenistic Period*, Fortress Press, 1975, pp. 58–106.

15. David A. Fiensy, 'The Composition of the Jerusalem Church', in *The Book of Acts in its First Century Setting, vol. IV: Palestinian Setting*, Eerdmans, 1995, pp. 213–36; see especially pp. 230–34.

16. The New Testament itself provides evidence for Greek-speaking synagogues in Jerusalem (Acts 6:9). In addition to Hengel's volume (see note 14 above), see Rainer Riesner, 'Synagogues in Jerusalem', in *The Book of Acts in its First Century Setting, vol. IV: Palestinian Setting*, pp. 179–210.

17. Meier, *A Marginal Jew*, vol. I, p. 268.

18. Paul Barnett, *The Birth of Christianity: The First Twenty Years*, Eerdmans, 2005, p. 113.

19. On this see Werner Kelber, *The Oral and Written Gospel*, Fortress Press, 1983, pp. 27, 50–51.

20. James D. G. Dunn, *Jesus Remembered*, Eerdmans, 2003, pp. 173–254.

21. Richard Bauckham, *Jesus and the Eyewitnesses: The Gospels as Eyewitness Testimony*, Eerdmans, 2006, pp. 240–318.

22. In addition to Bauckham, the evidence is explored in detail in Barnett, *The Birth of Christianity*, pp. 111–37. Key passages include 1 Corinthians 11:2; 15:1–3; 1 Thessalonians 4:1; Acts 2:42; 20:27–31; and Jude 3.

23. For an excellent introduction to this important topic see James H. Charlesworth (ed.), *Jesus and Archaeology*, Eerdmans, 2006.

24. Details of the Siloam pool are reported in Urban C. von Wahlde, 'Archaeology and John's Gospel', in Charlesworth (ed.), *Jesus and Archaeology*, pp. 568–70.

25. Burton Mack, *A Myth of Innocence: Mark and Christian Origins*, Fortress Press, 1988, pp. 67–74, 179–92. He has been followed in part by John Dominic Crossan, *The Historical Jesus*, HarperSanFrancisco, 1991.

26. For scholarly criticism of the Cynic-Jesus theory see N. T. Wright, *Jesus and the Victory of God*, Fortress Press, 1996, pp. 66–74; James D. G. Dunn, *Jesus Remembered*, Eerdmans, 2003, pp. 293–302; Sean Freyne, *Jesus, a Jewish Galilean: a New Reading of the Jesus Story*, T. & T. Clark, 2005, pp. 136–37.

27. Stanton, *The Gospels and Jesus*, 2nd edition, p. 295.

The Good Samaritan

1. James H. Charlesworth, *The Historical Jesus: An Essential Guide*, Abingdon Press, 2008, p. 25.

Ritual baths and vessels

1. James H. Charlesworth, *The Historical Jesus: An Essential Guide*, Abingdon Press, 2008, p. 25.

The gospel in Greek

1. The evidence for the two groups (Aramaic-speaking Christian Jews and Greek-speaking Christian Jews) is found in Acts 6:1–7. The events recorded here belong to the first year or two after the crucifixion.

2. So also Graham Stanton, *The Gospels and Jesus*, 2nd edition, Oxford University Press, 2003, p. 176. Professor Geza Vermes of Oxford University is simply mistaken when he states without argument: 'Since Jesus did not record his message in writing, it had to be handed down by his disciples orally, first in Aramaic and later in Greek when the evangelization moved outside Palestine among Jews and Gentiles who spoke Greek': Geza Vermes, *The Authentic Gospel of Jesus*, Penguin, 2003, p. 375.

How memories are retold

1. Bauckham, *Jesus and the Eyewitnesses*, pp. 319–57.

Conclusion: *Probability and Proof*

1. A watershed book on the limits of science and the 'faith commitments' undergirding the scientific method was written years ago by distinguished physical chemist, philosopher and Fellow of the Royal Society of England Michael Polanyi, *Personal Knowledge: Towards a Post-Critical Philosophy*, University of Chicago Press, 1974.

2. R. G. Collingwood, *The Idea of History*, Oxford University Press, 2005, pp. 251–52.

3. John P. Meier, *A Marginal Jew: Rethinking the Historical Jesus*, vol. I, Doubleday, 1991, p. 185.

Bibliography

Akenson, Donald Harman, *Saint Saul: A Skeleton Key to the Historical Jesus*, Oxford University Press, 2000.

Alexander, Loveday, 'What is a Gospel?', in Stephen C. Barton (ed.), *The Cambridge Companion to the Gospels*, Cambridge University Press, 2006, pp. 13–33.

Allison, Dale C., *Jesus of Nazareth: Millenarian Prophet*, Fortress Press, 1998.

Archer, Jeffrey, *The Gospel According to Judas, by Benjamin Iscariot*, Macmillan, 2007.

Bagatti, Bellarmino, *Excavations in Nazareth*, vol. I, Franciscan Printing Press, 1969.

Bammel, Ernst, 'A New Variant Form of the Testimonium Flavianum', *Judaica*, WUNT 37, Mohr Siebeck, 1987, pp. 190–93.

Barnett, Paul, *The Birth of Christianity: The First Twenty Years*, Eerdmans, 2005.

Bauckham, Richard, *Gospel Women: Studies in the Named Women in the Gospels*, Eerdmans, 2002, pp. 213–17.

—— 'James and the Jerusalem Community', in O. Skarsaune and R. Hvalvik (eds.), *Jewish Believers in Jesus: The Early Centuries*, Hendrickson, 2007, pp. 55–95.

—— *Jesus and the Eyewitnesses: The Gospels as Eyewitness Testimony*, Eerdmans, 2006.

—— *Jude and the Relatives of Jesus in the Early Church*, T. & T. Clark, 1990.

Betz, Otto, 'The Essenes', in *The Cambridge History of Judaism*, vol. III, edited by William Horbury *et al.*: *The Early Roman Period*, Cambridge University Press, 2001, pp. 444–70.

—— 'Jesus and the Temple Scroll', in James H. Charlesworth (ed.), *Jesus and the Dead Sea Scrolls*, Doubleday, 1992, pp. 75–103.

Black, Matthew, *An Aramaic Approach to the Gospels and Acts*, Clarendon Press, 1946.

Blomberg, Craig L., *Contagious Holiness: Jesus' Meals with Sinners*, InterVarsity Press, 2005.

Bock, Darrell L., *Luke 1:1 – 9:50*, *Baker Exegetical Commentary on the New Testament*, Baker, 1994.

Borg, Marcus J., *Jesus: A New Vision: Spirit, Culture, and the Life of Discipleship*, HarperCollins, 1991.

Bornkam, Günther, *Jesus of Nazareth*, Hodder & Stoughton, 1960.

Brakke, David, 'The Gnostics and Their Opponents', in *The Cambridge History of Christianity*, vol. I, edited by Margaret M. Mitchell and Frances M. Young: *Origins to Constantine*, Cambridge University Press, 2006, pp. 245–60.

Brandon, S. G. F., *Jesus and the Zealots*, Manchester University Press, 1967.

—— 'The Testimonium Flavium', *History Today* 19, 1969, pp. 26–42.

Brown, Dan, *The Da Vinci Code*, Bantam Press, 2003.

Brown, R. E., *The Birth of the Messiah*, Cassell & Collier Macmillan, 1977.

—— *The Death of the Messiah: From Gethsemane to the Grave*, 2 volumes, Doubleday, 1994.

Bultmann, Rudolf, *The History of the Synoptic Tradition*, Blackwell, 1972. (The original German edition was published in 1921.)

—— *Theology of the New Testament*, 2 volumes, Scribner, 1951–55.

Burkitt, F. C., 'Josephus and Christ', *Theologisch Tijdschrift* 47, 1913, pp. 135–44.

Burridge, Richard, *What are the Gospels? A Comparison With Graeco-Roman Biography*, Cambridge University Press, 1992.

Byrskog, Samuel, *Story as History, History as Story: The Gospel Tradition in the Context of Ancient Oral History*, Brill Academic Publishers, 2002.

Charlesworth, James H., 'The Dead Sea Scrolls and the Historical Jesus', in James H. Charlesworth (ed.), *Jesus and the Dead Sea Scrolls*, Doubleday, 1992, pp. 1–74.

—— *The Historical Jesus: An Essential Guide*, Abingdon Press, 2008.

—— *Jesus Within Judaism: New Light From Exciting Archaeological Discoveries*, Doubleday, 1988.

Charlesworth, James H. (ed.), *Jesus and Archaeology*, Eerdmans, 2006.

—— *Jesus' Jewishness: Exploring the Place of*

Jesus within Early Judaism, Crossroad Publishing, 1991.

Chilton, Bruce, 'Friends and Enemies', in Marcus Bockmuehl (ed.), *The Cambridge Companion to Jesus*, Cambridge University Press, 2001, pp. 72–86.

—— *Rabbi Jesus: An Intimate Biography*, Doubleday, 2000.

Chin, Catherine M., 'Rhetorical Practice in the Chreia Elaboration of Mara bar Serapion', *Hugoye: Journal of Syriac Studies*, 9/2, 2006, p. 21.

Clarke, G. W., 'The Origins and Spread of Christianity', in *The Cambridge Ancient History*, vol. X, edited by Alan K. Bowman *et al.: The Augustan Empire, 43 BC–AD 69*, Cambridge University Press, 1996, pp. 848–72.

Collingwood, R. G., *The Idea of History*, Oxford University Press, 2005.

Crossan, John Dominic, *The Historical Jesus*, HarperSanFrancisco, 1991.

—— *Jesus: A Revolutionary Biography*. HarperSanFrancisco, 1994.

Cureton, W., *Spicilegium Syriacum*, London: Francis and John Rivington, 1855, pp. 43–48 (Syriac), 70–76 (English).

Davies, W. D., and Allison, Dale C., *The Gospel According to Saint Matthew*, 3 volumes, T. & T. Clark, 1988–97.

Davies, W. D., and Sanders, E. P., 'Jesus: from the Jewish Point of View', in *The Cambridge History of Judaism*, vol. III, edited by William Horbury *et al.: The Early Roman Period*, Cambridge University Press, 2001, pp. 618–77.

Dawkins, Richard, *The God Delusion*, Bantam Press, 2006.

Deines, Roland, 'Martin Hengel: A Life in Service of Christology', *Tyndale Bulletin* 58/1, 2007, pp. 26–42.

Dickson, John, *The Christ Files: How Historians Know What They Know about Jesus*, Blue Bottle Books, 2005.

—— 'Gaffney's Gaffs on the Historical Jesus', *Australian Rationalist* 73, 2006, pp. 51–52.

—— *Spectator's Guide to World Religions: An Introduction to the Big Five*, Blue Bottle Books, 2004.

—— *James: The Wisdom of the Brother of Jesus*, Aquila Press, 2006.

—— 'Gospel as News: euaggel- from Aristophanes to the Apostle Paul', *New Testament Studies* 51/2, 2005, pp. 221–30.

—— *Mission-Commitment in Ancient Judaism and in the Pauline Communities*, WUNT II 159, Mohr Siebeck, 2003, 153–77.

Dornseiff, F., 'Zum Testimonium Flavium', *Zeitschrift für die neutestamentliche Wissenschaft* 46, 1955, pp. 245–50.

Dungan, David, *A History of the Synoptic Problem*, Doubleday, 1999.

Dunn, James D. G., *The Evidence for Jesus: The Impact of Scholarship on Our Understanding of How Christianity Began*, SCM Press, 1985.

—— *Jesus Remembered*, Eerdmans, 2003.

—— 'Pharisees, Sinners and Jesus', in Peder Borgen and Jacob Neusner (eds.), *The Social World of Formative Christianity and Judaism*, Fortress Press, 1988, pp. 264–89.

Ehrman, Bart D., *Misquoting Jesus: The Story Behind Who Changed the Bible and Why*, HarperSanFrancisco, 2005.

Evans, Craig A., 'Authenticating the Activities of Jesus', in Bruce Chilton and C. A. Evans (eds.), *Authenticating the Activities of Jesus*, Brill, 1999, pp. 3–29.

—— 'Context, Family and Formation', in Marcus Bockmuehl (ed.), *The Cambridge Companion to Jesus*, Cambridge University Press, 2001, pp. 13–15.

—— 'Hillel, House of', in *Dictionary of New Testament Background*, Inter-Varsity Press,, 2000, pp. 496–8.

—— *Life of Jesus Research: An Annotated Bibliography*, Brill, 1989.

—— *Mark 8:27 – 16:20*, Word Biblical Commentary, vol. 34b, Thomas Nelson, 2001.

—— *Noncanonical Writings and New Testament Interpretation*, Hendrickson, 1992.

—— 'Opposition to the Temple: Jesus and the Dead Sea Scrolls', in James H.

Charlesworth (ed.), *Jesus and the Dead Sea* Scrolls, Doubleday, 1992, pp. 235–53.

Evans, Craig A. (ed.), *Encyclopedia of the Historical Jesus*, Routledge, 2007.

Evans, C. F., *Saint Luke*, SCM, 1993.

Evans, C. S., *The Historical Christ and the Jesus of Faith: The Incarnational Narrative as History*, Clarendon Press, 1996.

Feldman, Louis H., 'The Testimonium Flavium: The State of the Question', in R. F. Berkey and S. A. Edwards (eds.), *Christological Perspectives*, Pilgrim, 1982, pp. 179–99, 288–93.

Ferguson, J., *The Religions of the Roman Empire*, Cornell University Press, 1970.

Fiensy, David A., 'The Composition of the Jerusalem Church', in *The Book of Acts in its First Century Setting*, vol. IV: *Palestinian Setting*, Eerdmans, 1995, pp. 213–36.

Fitzmyer, Joseph A., *The Gospel According to Luke*, 2 volumes, *The Anchor Bible* 28–28a, Doubleday, 1970, 1985.

—— *The Semitic Background of the New Testament*, combined edition of *Essays on the Semitic Background of the New Testament* and *A Wandering Aramean: Collected Aramaic Essays*, Eerdmans and Dove, 1997.

Flusser, David, 'Jesus, His Ancestry and the Commandment to Love', in James H. Charlesworth (ed.), *Jesus' Jewishness*, Crossroad, 1991, pp. 153–76.

Fortna, Robert T., *The Gospel of Signs*, Cambridge University Press, 1970.

Fowl, S. E., 'The Gospels and "the Historical Jesus"', in Stephen C. Barton (ed.), *The Cambridge Companion to the Gospels*, Cambridge University Press, 2006, pp. 76–96.

France, R. T., and Wenham, David (eds.), *Gospel Perspectives*, vol. III: *Studies in Midrash and Historiography*, Wipf & Stock, 2003.

Fredriksen, Paula, *Jesus of Nazareth: King of the Jews*, Vintage Books, 2000.

Freyne, Sean, *Jesus, a Jewish Galilean: A New Reading of the Jesus-Story*. T. & T. Clark, 2005.

Fuchs, Ernst, *Studies of the Historical Jesus*. SCM, 1964.

Funk, Robert W., *The Acts of Jesus: The Search for the Authentic Deeds of Jesus*, HarperSanFrancisco, 1998.

Funk, Robert W., and Hoover, Roy W. (eds.), *The Five Gospels: The Search for the Authentic Words of Jesus*, Macmillan, 1993.

Gaffney, Chris, 'The Origins of Christianity: From Jewish Revolution to a State Religion', *Australian Rationalist* 71, 2005, pp. 21–27

Gerhardsson, Birger, *The Reliability of the Gospel Tradition*, Hendrickson, 2001.

Goulder, M. D., *Midrash and Lection in Matthew*, London: SPCK, 1974.

Guelich, R. A., *Mark 1:1 – 8:26*, Word Biblical Commentary, vol. 34a, Word Publishers, 1989.

Hagner, Donald A., *Matthew 1–13*, Word Biblical Commentary 33a, Thomas Nelson, 1993.

Harris, William V., *Ancient Literacy*, Harvard University Press, 1989.

Hendin, D., *Guide to Biblical Coins*, 4th edition, Amphora, 2001.

Hengel, Martin, *Acts and the History of Earliest Christianity*, Wipf & Stock, 2003.

—— *The Atonement: The Origins of the Doctrine in the New Testament*, Wipf & Stock, 2007.

—— *The Charismatic Leader and His Followers*, Wipf & Stock, 2005.

—— *Crucifixion in the ancient world and the folly of the message of the cross*, Fortress Press, 1977.

—— *The Four Gospels and the One Gospel of Jesus Christ*, Trinity Press, 2000.

—— *Judaism and Hellenism: Studies in Their Encounter in Palestine During the Early Hellenistic Period*, Fortress Press, 1975.

—— *The Son of God: The Origin of Christology and the History of Jewish Hellenistic Religion*, Wipf & Stock, 2007.

—— *The Zealots*, T. & T. Clark, 1989.

Hengel, Martin, with Bailey, D. P., 'The Effective History of Isaiah 53 in the Pre-Christian Period', in Bernd Janowski and Peter Stuhlmacher (eds.), *The Suffering Servant: Isaiah 53 in Jewish and Christian Sources*, Eerdmans, 2004. pp. 75–146.

Hitchens, Christopher, *God is Not Great: How Religion Poisons Everything*, Twelve, 2007.

Holtzmann, H. J., *Die synoptischen Evangelien*, Engelmann, 1863.

Horbury, William, 'The Benediction of the *minim* and early Jewish-Christian Controversy', in *Jews and Christians in Contact and Controversy*, T. & T. Clark, 1998, pp. 67–110.

Horsley, R. A., and Silberman, N. A., *The Message and the Kingdom: How Jesus and Paul Ignited a Revolution and Transformed the Ancient World*, Grosset/Putnam, 1997.

Houston, J., *Reported Miracles: A Critique of Hume*, Cambridge University Press, 1994.

Hurtado, Larry, *How on Earth Did Jesus Become a God? Historical Questions about Earliest Devotion to Jesus*, Eerdmans, 2005.

Isser, Stanley, 'The Samaritans and Their Sects', in *The Cambridge History of Judaism*, vol. III, edited by William Horbury *et al.*: *The Early Roman Period*, Cambridge University Press, 2001, pp. 569–95.

Jenkins, Philip, *Hidden Gospels: How the Search for Jesus Lost its Way*, Oxford University Press, 2001.

Jeremias, Joachim, *The Rediscovery of Bethesda, John 5:2*, New Testament Archaeology Monographs 1, Southern Baptist Theological Seminary, 1966.

Johnson, Luke Timothy, *The Real Jesus*, HarperCollins, 1996.

Käsemann, Ernst, *Essays on New Testament Themes*, SCM, 1964.

Kee, H. C., *What Can We Know about Jesus?* Cambridge University Press, 1990.

Kelber, Werner, *The Oral and Written Gospel*, Fortress Press, 1983.

Klausner, Joseph, *Jesus of Nazareth: His Life, Times, and Teaching*, Menorah Publishing, 1925.

Krieger, N., 'Fiktive Orte der Johannestaufe', *Zeitschrift für die Neutestamentliche Wissenschaft und die Kunde der Älteren Kirche* 45, 1954, pp. 121–23.

Langer, Lawrence L., *Holocaust Testimonies: The Ruins of Memory*, Yale University Press, 1991.

Lüdemann, Gerd, *Jesus after Two Thousand Years: What He Really Said and Did*, SCM, 2000.

—— *What Really Happened to Jesus: A Historical Approach to the Resurrection*, Westminster John Knox Press, 1995.

Mack, Burton, *A Myth of Innocence: Mark and Christian Origins*, Fortress Press, 1988.

Marsh, John, *The Gospel of Saint John*, Penguin Books, 1968.

Marshall, I. Howard, *The Gospel of Luke*, New International Commentary on the New Testament, Eerdmans, 1978.

Meier, John P., *A Marginal Jew: Rethinking the Historical Jesus*, 3 volumes, Doubleday, 1991–2001.

—— 'Reflections on Jesus-of-History Research Today', in James H. Charlesworth (ed.), *Jesus' Jewishness*, Crossroad, 1991, pp. 84–107.

Metzger, Bruce M., *The Canon of the New Testament: Its Origin, Development and Significance*, Oxford University Press, 1997.

Meyer, Ben F., *The Aims of Jesus*, SCM, 1979.

Neill, Stephen, *The Interpretation of the New Testament, 1861–1986*, Oxford University Press, 1964; 2nd revised edition, edited by Tom Wright, 1988.

Neusner, Jacob, *From Politics to Piety: The Emergence of Pharisaic Judaism*, Englewood Cliffs, 1973.

Onfray, Michel, *The Atheist Manifesto*, Arcade Publishing, 2005.

Paffenroth, Kim, *The Story of Jesus according to L, Journal for the Study of the New Testament Supplement Series 147*, Sheffield Academic Press, 1997.

Perkins, Pheme, *Jesus as Teacher*, Cambridge University Press, 1990.

Perrin, Norman, *Rediscovering the Teaching of Jesus*, SCM, 1967.

Petzke, G., *Die Traditionen über Apollonius von Tyana und das Neue Testament*, Brill, 1970.

Phipps, William E., *Was Jesus Married? The Distortion of Sexuality in the Christian Tradition*, Harper & Row, 1970.

Pines, Shlomo, *An Arabic Version of the Testimonium Flavianum and Its Implications*, Israel Academy of Sciences and Humanities, 1971.

Polanyi, Michael, *Personal Knowledge: Towards a Post-Critical Philosophy*, University of Chicago Press, 1974.

Powell, M. A., *Jesus as a Figure of History: How Modern Historians View the Man from Galilee*, Westminster John Knox Press, 1998.

Reimarus, *Fragments*, edited by C. H. Talbert, Fortress Press, 1971.

Reisberg, Daniel, and Heuer, Friderike, 'Memory for Emotional Events', in Daniel Reisberg and Paula Hertel (eds.), *Memory and Emotion*, Oxford University Press, 2004, pp. 3–41.

Renan, Ernest, *The Life of Jesus*, Trubner, 1864.

Riesner, Rainer, *Paul's Early Period: Chronology, Mission Strategy, Theology*, Eerdmans, 1998.

—— 'Synagogues in Jerusalem', in *The Book of*

Acts in Its First Century Setting, vol. IV: *Palestinian Setting*, Eerdmans, 1995.

Rousée, J. M., 'Chroniques Archéologiques', *Revue Biblique* 69, 1962, pp. 107–109.

Rudolph, Kurt, 'Gnosticism', in *The Anchor Bible Dictionary*, vol. II, Doubleday, 1992, pp. 1033–44.

Sanders, E. P., *The Historical Figure of Jesus*, Penguin Books, 1993.

—— *Jesus and Judaism*, Fortress Press, 1985.

—— *Judaism: Practice and Belief, 63 BC–66 CE*, SCM Press, 1992.

Schaper, Joachim L. W., 'The Pharisees', in *The Cambridge History of Judaism*, vol. III, edited by William Horbury *et al.*: *The Early Roman Period*, Cambridge University Press, 2001, pp. 402–27.

Schneemelcher, Wilhelm (ed.), *New Testament Apocrypha*, 2 volumes, James Clarke & Co., 1991–2.

Schurer, Emil, revised and edited by Geza Vermes, Fergus Millar and Martin Goodman, *The History of the Jewish People in the Age of Jesus Christ*, vol. I, pt. 1, T. & T. Clark, 1987.

Schweitzer, Albert, *The Quest of the Historical Jesus*, Dover, 2005.

Spong, John Shelby, *Jesus for the Non-Religious*. HarperCollins, 2007.

Stanton, Graham, *The Gospels and Jesus*, 2nd edition, Oxford University Press, 2003.

—— *Jesus of Nazareth in New Testament Preaching*, Cambridge University Press, 1974.

—— 'Message and Miracles', in Marcus Bockmuehl (ed.), *The Cambridge Companion to Jesus*, Cambridge University Press, 2001, pp. 56–71.

Strauss, David Friedrich, *The Life of Jesus Critically Examined*, reissued SCM, 1973.

Stuhlmacher, Peter, *Jesus of Nazareth, Christ of Faith*, Hendrickson, 1993.

Theissen, Gerd, and Merz, Annette, *The Historical Jesus: A Comprehensive Guide*, Fortress Press, 1998.

Tuckett, Christopher, 'Sources and Methods', in *The Cambridge Companion to Jesus*, ed. Marcus Bockmuehl, Cambridge University Press, 2001, pp. 121–37.

Van Voorst, Robert E., *Jesus Outside the New Testament: An Introduction to the Ancient Evidence*, Eerdmans, 2000.

Vermes, Geza, *The Authentic Gospel of Jesus*, Penguin, 2003.

—— *Jesus the Jew: A Historian's Reading of the Gospels*, Collins, 1973.

—— 'The Jesus Notice of Josephus Re-examined', *Journal of Jewish Studies* 38, 1987, pp. 1–10.

von Wahlde, Urban C., 'Archaeology and John's Gospel', in James H. Charlesworth (ed.), *Jesus and Archaeology*, Eerdmans, 2006, pp. 523–86.

Wansbrough, H. (ed.), *Jesus and the Oral Gospel Tradition*, Sheffield Academic Press, 1991.

Wells, George A., *Did Jesus Exist?* Prometheus Books, 1975.

Wenham, David, *Paul: Follower of Jesus or Founder of Christianity?* Eerdmans,1995.

Wolterstorff, Nicholas, *Reason within the Bounds of Religion*, 2nd edition, Eerdmans, 1999.

Wrede, William, *The Messianic Secret*, James Clarke, 1971.

Wright, N. T., *Jesus and the Victory of God*, Fortress Press, 1996.

—— *Judas and the Gospel of Jesus*, SPCK, 2006.

—— *The New Testament and the People of God*, Fortress Press, 1992.

—— 'Quest for the Historical Jesus', in *The Anchor Bible Dictionary*, vol. III, Doubleday, 1992, pp. 796–802

—— *The Resurrection of the Son of God*, SPCK, 2003.

Wright, R. B., 'Psalms of Solomon', in James H. Charlesworth (ed.), The Old Testament Pseudepigrapha, vol. II, Doubleday, 1985, pp. 639–70

Zeitlin, Solomon, 'The Christ Passage in Josephus', *Jewish Quarterly Review* 18, 1927–8, pp. 231–55.

Acknowledgments

Alamy: p. 154 Israel Images

Allan Dowthwaite: pp. 28l, 45, 48, 53, 71, 79t, 98, 138, 141, 147, 149

British Library: p. 94 © The British Library Board, shelf mark Add.43725 f.262

Corbis: pp. 9, 137 Alinari Archives; pp. 14, 114 Philadelphia Museum of Art; p. 22 Bettmann; pp. 23, 25 Karl-Heinz Haenel; p. 26 Jon Hicks; p. 29 Atlantide Phototravel; p. 31 Dr. John C. Trever, PhD.; pp. 36, 37 Richard T. Nowitz; pp. 101, 119 The Gallery Collection; p. 106, 116 Araldo de Luca; p. 129 North Carolina Museum of Art; p. 135 Stefano Bianchetti; p. 142 Brooklyn Museum; p. 145 Alexander Burkatovski

Getty: p. 47 National Geographic; p. 50 Karen Bleier/AFP; p. 52 Jean Bourdichon/The Bridgeman Art Library; p. 62 Alfred Eisenstaedt/Time & Life Pictures; p. 81 Mihaly Munkacsy/The Bridgeman Art Library; p. 92 Bob Thomas/Popperfoto; pp. 86, 96, 102 Bridgeman Art Library; p. 131 Ridolfo Ghirlandalo/Bridgeman Art Library

John Dickson: pp. 11, 34, 35, 46, 64, 79, 150

Macquarie Papyri Research and Development Committee: p. 113 (both)

Mal Hamilton: pp. 42–43, 54, 69, 72, 73, 87, 133, 139,

Paul Moss: pp. 109, 130, 143, 151

Photolibrary: pp. 60, 63 E&E Image Library; pp. 122, 127 Fred de Noyelle

Scala: p. 75 © 1990 Photo Scala, Florence

Topfoto: pp. 13, 16, 18, 20, 66 The Granger Collection; p. 24 Ullsteinbild

Zev Radovan: p. 41

Richard Watts (Total Media Services): pp. 39, 58, 68, 93,

Lion Hudson

Commissioning editor: Paul Clifford

Project editor: Miranda Powell

Proofreaders: Rachel Ashley-Pain / Elizabeth Evans

Designer: Jonathan Roberts

Picture researcher: Jenny Ward

Production manager: Kylie Ord